With 48 black-and-white illustrations

Marya Mannes has devoted her life as a writer to questioning common myths and assumptions in the light of observed realities and the imperative need for change.

Very much a woman, she has nevertheless rejected the traditional "role" assigned to women, and consistently attacked stereotypes, hypocrisy, and pretence in every area of life.

This book is her autobiography: searching, vulnerable, spirited, and often humorous. She describes her childhood in an uncommon family—her musician parents founded the Mannes College of Music, her musician brother co-invented the Kodachrome process—and her equally uncommon education.

With unsparing candor she examines her marriages and her relations with men, and her chequered and

Television, and her adaptation of her novel *They* for TV was repeated three times on this network, followed in the Spring of 1971 by her first TV documentary *Guests on This Planet.*

Out of My Time

By Marya Mannes

OUT OF MY TIME

THEY

BUT WILL IT SELL?

THE NEW YORK I KNOW

MORE IN ANGER

MESSAGE FROM A STRANGER

with Robert Osborn

SUBVERSE: RHYMES FOR OUR TIMES

Out of My Time

Marya Mannes

Doubleday & Company, Inc.
Garden City, New York

PHOTOGRAPH CREDITS

Plates 1–17, 23, 26, 27, 33, 37 Private collection of Marya Mannes
Plate 22 Photograph by ALFREDO VALENTE
Plates 24–25 VOGUE photographs by Cecil Beaton; Copyright © 1933, 1961 by The Condé Nast Publications Inc.
Plates 34–36 VOGUE photographs by Marya Mannes; Copyright © 1946 by The Condé Nast Publications Inc.
Plate 38 PETER SEKAER
Plate 39 Steve Schapiro, LIFE Magazine © Time Inc.

Library of Congress Catalog Card Number 70–168284

Printed in the United States of America

To my son
with love and respect

1971

Preface

Wohleben is stumbling about the craters of the moon. They surround him on all sides, cold and mournful pits and ranges, lead-gray with pitch-black crevices and chromium highlights. The air about him has the substanceless pure radiance of a neon light, in white-violet. With his helmet and his suit, bulky with apparatus, and his slow, intent movements, Wohleben looks much like a diver on the sea floor. He keeps lifting his clumsy head to look at a big planet in the eastern sky; and when he does so, you can see the spread of lips and the glint of teeth under the helmet.

Wohleben existed in my imagination forty years ago. He was part of a book I was writing then. Though it was neither finished nor published, he will weave in and out of this story because Wohleben and I were very close.

Though he would never confess it, one motive impelled all of Wohleben's exploits. One obsession that made him climb the unclimbed Kanchenjunga, fly the first plane that could hover indefinitely at any altitude, explore the subterranean oceans of the North Pole and, finally, rocket to the moon. Wohleben was looking for the ghosts of his youth.

He was hardly the first. The trip is a well-traveled route; a tourist excursion for some, an agonized search for others. Why am I as I am? Why do I do as I do?

Why, in this case, did the explorer have to be a man, when he was palpably myself? What forms a woman whose dreams have no gender? What makes a spiritual hermaphrodite?

Wohleben was forty-five now. At thirty he had already begun to review his life with great impersonality, checking its merits and demerits. And as he reviewed it, a new conception of the human being came to him, almost as a vision. He saw himself as the outermost egg of one of those wooden eggs the Russians once made for children. Within the outer egg was a smaller egg, within that a still smaller, within that a smaller, and so on until the carpenter's skill was exhausted. In this way, he, Wohleben, at thirty incorporated at least four ghosts of constantly diminishing size.

And so on, to the small egg of self, a boy of two who found in a smooth brass button that glinted in the sun "a violent pleasure in the holding of it."

A ghost, thought Wohleben, was what reality left behind;

and bore to this reality the same relation that a beam of light bears to its source.

Wohleben loved these ghosts, missed them, wanted them—and set out to look for them. But it was not till he was forty-five and wandering clumsily among the lunar crevasses that the thought came, with a contraction of his heart: "Then I am only a reality whose ghost lives in the shell of some superman. And it is him I should be looking for!"

Here we diverge. I do not love all my ghosts, and miss very few. It is too late in any case to inhabit, let alone be, that final super-being, the super-egg.

What's more I did not deliberately summon my ghosts. They issued from cartons and trunks long stored away and forgotten, opened only to spare others the burden of their real and intangible weight after my death.

In so doing, barely a year ago, I not only found Wohleben but evidence of an exploration as difficult and at times as hazardous as his by a human being who happens to be a woman. Since the woman is also a writer, beginning at the age of six to set down what she saw and felt and imagined, the record is copious, sometimes ludicrous, and always revealing. It will be quoted throughout these pages not because of literary value—often negligible or absent—but because of the reliability of the source, who, like Wohleben, was obsessed with curiosity and driven by visions. Out of the collective ghosts now summoned from six decades may emerge, hopefully, the reality of a woman who fought for the freedom to be herself long before the fight was formalized, and who—because she never rode a crest—often crested too soon or too late, with few looking.

Timing and arrogance are decisive factors in the successful use of talent. The first is a matter of instinct, the second part carapace and part self-hypnosis; the shell that protects, the ego that assumes, without question, that the talent possessed is not only unique but important, the particular vision demanding to be shared.

The shell I have never grown. Whether the arrogance is more apparent than actual is for the reader to judge.

I can only assert that if this book, unlike preceding ones, is concerned more with the origins and nature of self than with the major issues of society, it is not for the sake of self-advertisement: a charge (in this public age) to which I plead innocent. I have used this self, on the contrary, as a living specimen for others to inspect for clues to themselves.

The scalpel hurt: there was no anesthetic for deep incisions and tissue laid bare. But I felt it was necessary at this time to show, not by abstractions but by example, the dual nature of woman (as of man) that must be recognized where it exists, and also accepted, if we are to reach our long-delayed full growth as human beings.

Out
of My
Time

1.

Infants are interesting only to their parents. In the case of the smallest ghost, therefore, it should be sufficient to mention only those qualities in the small girl-child that still inhabit the grown woman.

Except for the brass button in the sun, which I can still feel and see, the evidence is part photographic—doting parents snapped their offspring in every stage of growth—and part hearsay.

The snapshots show a plump child with very light hair and very round and serious eyes. Between them her mother wrote that she was flirtatious, curious, temperamental, greedy for food, animals, water to swim in, fields of flowers, and, of course, attention. She ran, danced, made scenes when thwarted, melted when not.

It appears that she was quiet only when asleep; or on the pot, in moments of contemplation so prolonged that—on the testimony of her brother five years her senior—a new nurse finally picked her up by her hair and removed her, screaming. (The nurse was fired that night.)

At the age of three, the curiosity impelled her to drink a bottle of ink. Through the intervention of horrified parents and a doctor, who upended her and flushed her out, she survived.

So did the legend, repeated through several decades, that the ink had been coming out of her ever since.

In her father's autobiography, written three decades later, the only mention of the smallest ghost was that the family now included "a beautiful and obstreperous girl." By that time he had already had ample and sometimes unsettling evidence that his daughter could speak for herself.

• • •

This compulsive need to put down what I saw began with a diary given me on my first trip abroad at the age of five: the first of many such tours to Europe in which parental concerts alternated with family holidays.

In those earlier days we traveled four in a cabin. Of the three berths, Leopold and I shared one. With the steward's help a long wooden plank was placed on it thin side up and diagonally, halving it so that each of us could lie with our heads on the wide end and our feet on the narrow. This was tougher on him than on me since he was five years longer, but we maintained a decent truce under strict maternal edict. The days, in any case, were less constricted.

> The capten is rather a fat man. But he is short . . . I usually play on the uper sundeck. I clime the posts up it. I am just writing with my folding pentsil . . .

In Berlin my pentsil failed to record the sight of Kaiser Wilhelm the Second—*Pickelhaube,* cape, withered arm, and all—on the steps of the palace, but wrote about "too little lions who were only three months old . . . the nerss is a bulldog."

Slightly more pertinent was an entry made at Schandau to the effect that I saw "Mother's and Father's engaging house." Somewhat later my mother told me: "Your father asked me to marry him in Schandau, and when I asked him *why* he wanted to marry me, do you know what he said? 'Because I'm looking for the truth!' "

It took me ten more years to understand this.

The only entry in that first diary that rose above phonetic declaration was scrawled under a postcard of a glacier. "One day I saw a very big avalanche it was like thunder and it was very loude. But it was great."

A touch of Chaucer?

2.

In these years, starting at five, began the first conscious joy in belonging to an extraordinary family: three people to whom I owe whatever good inhabits my being, and whatever vulnerability has caught me, often, at odds with society and its succeeding molds, including today's.

My father, David Mannes, was a beautiful man. Beautiful in his visible person, "beautiful," too, in the way the young use the word. Tall, very thin, the aristocracy of his movements hardly suggested the background from which he sprung and the childhood in which he was formed. Only his eyes and his mouth, in repose or thought, were invested with the intrinsic sadness of his race, testament to endless wanderings and long rejection. He was subject to deep depressions from which only music, the vitality of his wife, and the presence of his children could lift him. He would tell me about them from the time I was six. He would assume that I understood whatever he said; and I did. Perhaps not wholly, at first, but increasingly.

He would tell me what he had seen and felt, about the divinity of man ("we all have it in us, we just have to find it"), he would talk about making music. All his life he would show me something new he had just discovered about the violin: a position of hand or arm that affected sound, a way of phrasing, a tension of body. At ninety, when all else was growing distant and dim, he would bring his violin to me and say "Listen: don't you think this sounds better?" raise the instrument to his chin, and with clear articulation play passages of Bach or Brahms.

At three he taught me to dance the polka, at four he lowered me, at the end of a hawser tied around my middle, into a lake, dunking me while I cried "More! More!" At ten he told me "You can be anything you want to be. Never set any limitations on yourself."

And he would tell me what little he knew about his origins. That his grandfather, Simon Mannes, was a journeyman baker, tramping all over German Poland and Prussia, baking as he went. That he came from an orthodox Jewish family but made many Christian friends. "I think this is a proof," my father wrote later as he would often tell me, "of his intelligence, for only the limited Jews want to wall themselves up with their own kind."

Simon the baker fathered Henry the baker, who was fairly well educated and had a small talent in drawing. But of what use was that, my father said, in feeding seven children, of which he was the youngest?

My grandfather Mannes married Nathalia Wittkowska of Wittkowo, Poland. She could neither read nor write because the early death of her mother forced her, as the only girl, to keep house for her father and brothers instead of going to school. Yet she grew up with a passion for music and an abiding hero worship of actors, poets, and statesmen, both fueled by the concerts and plays my grandfather took her to and the books he read to her when their work was done and their children put to bed.

My childhood memories of my Polish grandparents are brief but clear: two dear small white-haired people who made up in natural grace what they lacked in height, who were immaculately dressed, and who came every birthday to bring me white kid gloves—"Because she is a princess!" they told my parents. I never wore them because I hated gloves (shoes, girdles, bras, anything that constricted) throughout the years. But they were my first lesson in the kind of self-respect uncontaminated by external scales of worth. The word "underprivileged" had not entered the language.

Privileged, in any case, they were not: either in the Poland they left in 1870 on a sailing vessel that took forty-one days to reach New York or in their early struggle to survive here. My grandfather spent his first year working a twelve-hour shift in a basement bakery without ventilation or daylight. The resulting ill health forced him to find another job, this time with the help of a cousin, starting a second-hand clothing shop on Seventh Avenue.

My father was born—the last of five brothers and a sister—in the middle of what was then called the Tenderloin.

> Twenty-seventh Street from Sixth to Seventh Avenue [he wrote in his autobiography], was entirely given over to houses of prostitution. On three out of the four corners of every street were saloons—the kind with swing doors and sawdust and the smell of liquor and sweat coming

out of them—and the number of drunken bums lying about was such a natural thing that one took it as a matter of course. You just stepped around or over them. Police raids and evictions of our neighbors were frequent; and I remember these scantily clad, disheveled women being herded and driven off in police wagons, yelling and crying and struggling against the policemen. Fights between street gangs were almost a nightly experience and we used to keep indoors in terror of our lives. I suppose to some that surrounding evil might have held a romantic lure. But not to me. Not then or ever. I hate mess and confusion and squalor. It frightens me as a mob frightens me and leaves profound depression in its wake.

The school I went to at that time was no bulwark either against that depression or the squalor that caused it. Nor was it in any sense of the word an education. . . . The fact is, I had only four years of schooling in my entire life. And what schooling!

Public School 55 (at Twentieth Street and Sixth Avenue) was the background of miserable boyhood months. The hard benches, the crowded rooms, the fetid atmosphere, the spitting boys and tired, irritable teachers—these were no incentive to learning. The filth was indescribable (there was no plumbing whatsoever), and the heat and litter of the crowded basement yard at recess time made even that small oasis sordid. The end of the school day left me spent and wretched.

When he was not at school he was at home helping his mother in her endless duties, derided by his brothers for these "feminine activities." He was also providing his own education in the new store his father now ran, which bought and sold furniture, old china, and books.

These books attracted me, and I read, and somehow became absorbed in, many an old volume that I couldn't completely grasp. One of these was Renan's *Life of Christ,* in English of course; many were old Bibles. Until that time in Sunday school and during the Jewish holidays, my only history was the Old Testament, for which I felt no interest. I even fought against further knowledge of it.

So it was the New Testament which I read and read, and my love and enthusiasm for its central figure grew and grew. This experience was another profound impression, perhaps the most important of my entire life, and certainly the most sustaining.

But even before that, music had become an obsession. His first instrument was a series of wires stretched across a cigar box. When his parents bought him a small second-hand violin, he taught himself to play by ear. His first teacher was a man who heard him playing by an open window one summer day. He went to the front door and knocked, my grandmother opened it and saw a tall Negro who lifted his hat to her and, apologizing for interrupting, asked who the player was. He himself, he explained, was a violin teacher. My grandmother invited him in and showed him her youngest son. The stranger told them he felt the boy had talent, and would he care to have music lessons for 25 cents an hour? Mother and boy accepted with alacrity. "He was a wonderful man," said my father again and again, "and a fine musician. I owe him so much."

How this man's student became a distinguished musician —violinist, teacher, conductor—was part of our continuing dialogue and all of the story David Mannes was to write himself in his seventieth year: "Music Is My Faith."

I lived with this story too: it became part of me. So, of course, did the woman who left no such written testament.

My mother, Clara Damrosch, came from a very different world. She was born in Breslau, Germany (now Wroclaw, Poland), of an already distinguished musician, Leopold Damrosch, and of Helena von Heimburg, one of fourteen children of a *Junker* family that reached back in an unbroken line to the eleventh century.

Helena had cracked the mold of the good German Aryan female (*Kinder, Kirche,* and *Küche*) by becoming an opera singer—a mezzo-soprano of sufficient distinction to perform leading roles in Wagner operas at Weimar—and by marrying a Jew.

Through the encouragement of Franz Liszt, Leopold Damrosch had joined the orchestra at Weimar as concertmaster and it is no legend that he took one look at the tall regal blonde on the stage and committed himself to her for life.

I marveled that the same pattern repeated itself precisely decades later, when my father, playing with the first violins (he was later concertmaster) of the New York Symphony Orchestra, committed *himself* on sight to a fair young woman in the chorus. That this enthusiastic alto voice belonged to the sister of his conductor, Walter Damrosch, he did not then know. But no less acute an observer than Willa Cather, writing in the *Courier* in 1898 of Melba's last appearance at a gala Metropolitan concert, noted that "Mr. Mannes, the violinist, acquitted himself brilliantly and was warmly received. During the applause which followed his first number, he stood bowing up at Miss Damrosch, to whom he is engaged."

My mother, brought here as a baby, grew up in a highly cultivated home, where books and music and talk were staples as constant as food and wine, where the five surviving children, born to Helena after she left the stage, went to the best private schools, spoke fluent French and German as well as precise and expressive English, and had never been exposed to the squalors of street life so familiar to David Mannes.

Clara Damrosch lived in the adored shadow of her father and of her two brothers, Frank and Walter, who left in their new country lasting marks as musicians and educators.

Money was always short; standards were not. My mother went to an exacting girls' school run on Lycée principles, practiced piano and learned theory under the eyes of a stern matriarch and demanding father, and emerged as—well—a lady: a term she never used though clearly fulfilled. She was a musician who married a beautiful man who was also a musician, and that was that.

She was, as they called it then, "refined." She never used bad language, told dirty jokes, or discussed sex. And my father had learned to confine his earthy comments to the more appreciative audience of his children and male companions. One of his first jobs as youthful violinist was in a popular bawdy house of the time, and although his accounts of the wild doings there invariably included words like "sordid" and "those poor women" (or "coarse men"), it sounded fascinating.

Physically and emotionally, my parents could not have been more different. Against his long dark leanness, she was short, fine boned and inclined to plumpness until her final years. She had thin ashen hair and brilliant blue-green eyes that could—and did—shoot sparks; a radiant smile; and the nose, broken in a childhood bicycle fall, of a Roman matron.

She was positive where father was tentative, definite where he was vague, highly organized where he was not, dominant where he was passive, resistant where he was pliant.

My mother was good at everything she tackled except the domestic arts: these she never had to. In those days even musicians could afford servants to cook and clean, and living space for a female relative (in our case a lovely great-aunt) to run the household, or for long-term nurses who became part of the family. Mother was therefore free to pursue a musical talent equal and some said technically superior to my father's, in teaching and chamber music; to concern herself deeply with her two children and their growth; and to create an environment of charm and comfort on the modest budget all but the famous in music could allow.

Mistress of household accounts (money was both mystery and anathema to my father), she believed in spending what they made on the good things in life, which included travel and theater as well as food and wine, with the known consequence of starting from scratch every year in the savings account.

They both worked equally hard, animated by common standards, sustained by common devotions. Theirs was a total union in life and labor rare in marriage although, I have thought through the years, one of the few premises for marital success.

That this union should have produced a spiritual hermaphrodite in me should surprise no one. Each of them possessed an almost equal balance of male and female qualities while retaining, to a high degree, their sexual identities.

I grew up, in short, with none of the stereotypes of sex and sex roles which have so contracted the lives of most men and women, and with none of the hand-me-down limitations forced on children in the name of "normality," convention, or even love.

For that matter, I found the lives led in the homes of middle-class schoolmates not only abnormal but boring. No talk, no music, no books, no funny friends, no games. Just a father away at business, a mother fussing at food, and chatter of clothes and hair and boys that left me alien and remote.

The thought that of the two sexes one was intrinsically better than the other didn't cross my mind until I began to run after my older brother, Leopold. Much later, I grew strong enough to know that our paths were separate, if intellectually unequal. He was very close to genius.

• • •

Leopold Damrosch Mannes was born with great difficulty and nearly died five years before I appeared.

My memory of him during the next five years was dim; an older presence, in and out, who was—he made it abundantly clear thereafter—all too conscious of mine. This was not (I was later assured), due to jealousy at attention diverted from him to me. He was already a prodigy at four, playing piano by ear, talking fluently, beautiful for his auburn curls and big brown eyes, and adored by his parents.

Once I could wipe my chin and make declarative sentences, he could just tolerate me. Nuisance and underfoot though I might be, moreover, I was a willing experiment in education. He would lead and I would follow. Under his tutelage, buttressed by school, I became the second ghost.

• • •

Our home was a long and wandering apartment on Amsterdam Avenue and Seventy-fifth Street: three blocks from Riverside Park, two blocks from Central Park, one block from school, and three blocks from the subway station at Broadway and Seventy-second where Father went every day to reach the Third Street Settlement Music School where he taught and which he ultimately directed.

Actually it was two apartments joined together in a squared-off U. One long flange faced on Seventy-fifth Street, the short span fronted on Amsterdam and a warehouse, the other flange on a dark court except for the end, which was Leopold's domain.

The front door lead into a long corridor and parental territory: their bedroom; a den, covered with signed photographs of composers, performers, singers, conductors, with a desk; and a large bright corner room facing south and west where the music was made: dominated, of course, by a grand piano, and inhabited also by stands for chamber music and a plaster replica of the Winged Victory on a marble column. Window seats, sofas, and chairs lined the other three walls.

Heavy dark green velvet curtains separating this room from the others when Mother taught piano students, or rehearsed with Father, were otherwise parted. At five o'clock every weekday afternoon, my mother and I and our beautiful white Persian family cat would sit on the corner window seat to look for Father walking from the subway.

Everyday we tried to be first to cry "There he is!" the first to notice whether he looked tired or not. But Puff was always the first to get to the front door long before Father had even turned the key.

The dining room, facing Amsterdam, was overwhelmed by a towering sideboard of golden oak with a large round matching table and heavy chairs. None of us admired the wood, the design, or the color, but we got used to it because we had to use it. Besides, the table was the only place Leopold and I could do our written homework at night without impinging too closely upon each other. Periodically our great-aunt, Tante, would patrol the area, or my nurse, a room away, would keep her ears pricked for untoward sounds.

Beyond this dining room was a strange arrangement allocated to me. The front part, on Amsterdam, was a small sitting room with bookcases and places for toys. The back part, on a court, was another small room where I slept and kept my clothes.

The trouble was that the "public" corridor ran between these parts, with no doors to either. Leopold had to go through my domain to reach the long corridor that led to his; so did Tante and the nurse, in reverse, to get to the kitchen behind the dining room. It is possible that this was excellent training for public life, and it certainly didn't stop me from having private thoughts. It may also explain why—until this violent age—I hated shut doors, locked or unlocked, when I was alone.

In any case there were long hours when my brother was at school or my parents at work when I was free to sprawl, to read, to dream, and above all, to hang by my knees from a trapeze swung from the wide and doorless frame of my bedroom. I found this very comforting, and did it daily until well into my teens to the embarrassment and distress of my brother. By then he would sometimes lead schoolmates back into the pantry attached to his room and equipped for the early rituals and experiments that preceded the ultimate co-invention of Kodachrome. At least, that was the presumption. The reality might have been a cache of suggestive literature, but since Leopold was secretive to a degree, I never knew.

All the more reason, then, why he took a poor view of

having to take people past a half-clad sister, up-ended skirts obscuring her face and hair, long legs revealed while she swung lightly and meditatively back and forth.

In time this reached the upper court, with my father defending the right of the accused to swing in her own room, my mother pleading for a sense of common modesty, my brother adding that I was no treat to the boys. Since, through a staggering ignorance of sex, I couldn't have cared less what his schoolmates thought, I merely shrugged.

Again, I had never thought in terms of "girl" and "boy." For a while I did have dolls, but remember only one I invested with life: by giving her a book to read. I set her on my window seat, put the book in her lap, and turned a page whenever I remembered to. So that she wouldn't be bored, of course.

For that, except for fun outdoors, was all I wanted to do when I was alone: read, write, draw pictures. Read, gaze, dream. And later—a few years later—be someone else.

• • •

The word "tomboy" then was used, by men and women alike, with a deprecatory smile. It meant "you know, she's in that phase," or "give her time and she'll be a real girl."

The length of this phase so far as I was concerned worried my independent working mother more than my father. Even without Freud to prompt her, she feared I might not develop properly into a woman. I preferred the company of boys not because of their sex but because I wanted to do the things they did more than what most girls did. I wanted to climb, to race, to perform daring feats, to walk on narrow rails. I wanted to lead more than follow, swim faster than others, feel the delicious prickle of risk. I felt suffocated by strictly feminine absorptions. And as time went on, in every book I read, in every play I was taken to, it was never the woman—except for Joan of Arc—I wanted to be.

Always Lancelot, never Guinevere; Henry VIII, never (zounds!) his wives. Hamlet, of course; never, God help me, his mother or Ophelia. The men may have been rogues and murderers, but never idiots like their mooning women. I even rather liked Richard III, one of my roles.

My parents never knew just what, in my preadolescent days, they would find me playing. Hamlet they understood, impressed by the costume I managed to concoct out of black stockings and a black sweater and by an impassioned rendition of certain quotes. Richard alarmed them slightly. The costume was sinister enough: the same stockings but a feathered beret askew a contorted face, one shoulder hunched (hand dangling) while I limped and grimaced and hissed vile plots. These and other notable performances were given in front of the trapeze, and my public tried hard not to laugh. Leopold was once rebuked for giggling and once for shaking his head in hopeless derision. He made up for this by constructing a complete miniature theater with a wooden stage, a cardboard proscenium, flats movable through an intricate system of pulleys, and a curtain that drew. He cut little figures out of cardboard, set upright in wooden cases, from plays we both knew and allowed me to paint their faces and costumes as well as the proscenium arch. With rare benevolence, moreover, he let me choose the scenes and play most of the characters as he moved them back and forth across the stage. Even Caesar, dying.

These drew respectful audiences, augmented by cousins, guests, the cook, and anyone else interested in the art of theater. Together with my personal appearances in single roles, a marked tendency for high drama out of costume as well earned me the family title of "tragedy queen." It was not entirely complimentary, for the public intensity of my moods—rhapsody to despair—could be trying. Especially for Leopold, who loathed public displays of emotion.

They were, I am sure, much relieved when I transferred them at least in part to the written page in forms ranging from portentous and derivative verse to daily annals and Deep Thoughts, of which a few samples will be given in due course.

The tomboy obsessed with vision explains, of course, why Wohleben and myself were one. I have never climbed a glacier higher than fourteen thousand feet. But he and I were on the moon in the nineteen-thirties, where no women could possibly have been.

• • •

In the résumés everyone sooner or later has to fill out, my response to the query "Education" was simple: the Veltin School, New York City, 1912–23. Period. And indeed there I learned most of what I know of French and English classic literature and language, of Latin, of ancient and European history, of the nature of girls and teachers.

But the word "Home" belonged first; birth to eighteen years. Music was a total environment from infancy on; an ambience of sound felt if not perceived, perceived if not defined, by the smallest ear, through the thinnest skin, through walls and doors, sleeping and waking. Perhaps even through the womb, in prenatal fluid.

I was never a musician. Ten years of piano, augmented by theory, solfège, and counterpoint, confirmed not only a lack of performing talent but my own recognition that nothing I could possibly play would sound as it should. The sounds I heard from my mother and father through the heavy curtains or on a concert stage I could never attain, nor those of a brilliant brother playing alone. So as the years went on, I contented myself with improvisation when no one was listening, a flageolet on which I could pipe a wide range of tunes from Bach inventions to *L'Après-Midi d'un Faune,* and the conducting of innumerable scores at my seat in concert halls.

Correction: In 1917, in the third grade at school, our French principal, an ardent patriot, decreed that all students must take military drill. We were to wear blue serge bloomers and white middies, be issued wooden guns, and repair en masse to an armory twice a week.

With the strong support of my parents, I made loud my protest: I would not carry a gun. The headmistress compressed her lips (not for the last time) and said, "Well, you must do something for the Allied cause, my child!" I took a deep breath and said, "I will play the bugle."

I ran home with this news, which was not received with enthusiasm. First, they would have to buy a bugle. Second, they would have to listen to it. Third, I had no idea how to play it. But they were trapped. On the stringent condition that I would not practice or play while the others were doing either, or simply resting, I taught myself. Once I could vibrate my lips while spitting into the mouthpiece, all went well. Taps and reveille and simple alarums rang through the armory and helped our cause. I was even admired.

With that single triumph of my musical career, back to the point. During those years artists like Casals, Cortot, Harold Bauer, Jacques Thibaud, Artur Schnabel and many more came to our home to play chamber music with my parents; to eat, drink, or talk. The curtains were open then and I could watch while Leopold turned my mother's pages. Trios, quartets, sextets—Brahms, Mozart, Beethoven, Schubert, Fauré, Ravel—rang in my ears, pervaded my being. Even more, I could watch what happened to the faces of these musicians as they played: a transmutation clear even to a child.

One of my half-joking complaints to my family was that so many musicians were homely: usually short, with irregular faces and fuzzy hair and baggy clothes. When they played this strange thing happened: their intense absorption in what they loved made them somehow noble, beautiful.

I saw it even in my own parents, who were far from homely. My mother's face attained a pure serenity, my father's a special kind of virility. I could not explain it, I just saw it. As for my brother, it was the only time he shut his mouth. Usually it hung slightly open, possibly because he was too preoccupied to close it.

These were, I am sure, my earliest lessons in involvement: the devotion of human beings to something beyond themselves. This is doubtless why none of us were ever drawn to the business community, why talk of money seemed either incomprehensible, demeaning, or simply boring, and why—with the exception of Leopold, as coinventor with Leopold Godowsky of Kodachrome—we were never good at making it.

This view of business as a necessary evil softened as each of us in turn met business leaders of vision, liberality, and integrity. But the creative society—and that, of course, included scientists, scholars, statesmen, doctors, and lawyers who could think beyond the terms of their professions—was for each of us the essential ambience.

• • •

Music, words, and pictures—these were all part of a home education that must have accelerated my "formal" learning.

My father's three passions—none of them, needless to say,

spurred by his four years of school—were Christ, Lincoln, and George Bernard Shaw. The New Testament was a revelation to him, Lincoln his idol, and Shaw his delight.

I remember so well his impatience with the predominant view of Christ as "meek," the martyred divinity. "He was a *man,*" father insisted, "didn't he chase the moneylenders out of the temple? He was a man!" "A man of sorrows and acquainted with grief, yes," he went on, "but a fighter too!"

Walt Whitman came later. When we both caught up with him, especially in *When Lilacs Last in the Dooryard Bloom'd*, we wept again for Lincoln's death; and I still do.

A rebel himself, a searcher of new ways and ideas, Father relished Shaw's irreverance and iconoclasm; quoted passages on the freeing of women, on marriage, on religion, on the business mentality. He loved Shaw even more on stage, for he had a passion for theater and actors born decades earlier when he played at fourteen in the pit of the Union Square Theatre.

Because of his age and inexperience, the Musical Union could not allow him to be paid, but, he wrote:

p. 42 (Music is My Faith)

> My joy at being allowed to go the the theater every night and two matinees a week cannot be conceived. It was the happiest engagement of my life. I would be at the theater long before any of the orchestra came, walking on the stage, becoming acquainted with that mysterious life behind the scenes, the lifting and moving of scenery, the miraculous lighting of border gaslights by electric sparks, and the blinding glare of calcium light projectors.
>
> It was in my modest place in the orchestra of the Union Square Theatre that I heard the English language

spoken with a beauty strange and entrancing to me . . . So while the other musicians went under stage to play cards during the performance, I remained in the orchestra pit, listening enthralled every night . . .

I began reading in deadly earnest all the best there was in English literature, much to the displeasure of my parents who felt I was wasting my time on books "that were not true" when I had better, and much more to my profit, practice my violin.

My mother, however, remained the inveterate reader; in French as well as in English, in German too, although she had no great love for its literature. It was Tante mostly who read Goethe and Heine and Schiller aloud to me, translating what my *Kindersprache* could not imbibe and thus easing me gently into the language itself.

She also, poor darling, tried to explain the libretti of the Wagnerian operas to me, before and during intermissions in the family box. I thus acquired a very hazy intimation of what the heavy ladies and fur-bearing men were doing on stage, although during the interminable bellowings my small mind would wander either far afield, fasten on the tenor's stomach, or wonder why female singers had no waists. I hope she will never know that in spite of my illustrious Damrosch forbears and late kin, I find German opera very hard to watch, especially now that I have forgotten the story line except for Tristan and Isolde. That hit me later and with full force, when I learned what love, if not climax, was all about. Yet opera, with very few exceptions, was for me to be heard rather than seen. Finding the posturing and the plots often inane, I prefer great music straight.

The highlight, perhaps, in home education in literature

occurred during a summer at Chatham, on Cape Cod; saddened by Father's severe bout of melancholia and the sinister clouds of World War One.

Too depressed, too listless to play, Father would sit; brooding on failure, threading long pieces of twine or wool around pegs in what was then supposed to be therapy.

During the daytime Mother would practice, but without heart since she played without him; and my brother and I spent most of our time outdoors on separate pursuits with separate friends, swimming or sailing.

But the nights were a challenge to Mother, and as usual she rose to it. During the nearly three months we were there in the rented cottage, she read every novel of Charles Dickens out loud. She read well—her diction was beautiful —and even Father listened.

We sat before the fire and hardly moved. Often we watched her face as she read, for it was expressive and revealing. As she approached a sad passage her eyes would begin to fill and her lips quiver ever so slightly. Brutes that we were, all three of us would start saying "Here it comes!" or "There she goes!" and Mother, with a show of outrage, would stop reading, blow her nose, or wipe her eyes while we rolled, chortling, on the floor.

The crowning moment arrived when Little Dorrit, whom we all thought idiotic, died; and sure enough we caught Mother in the old reflex, and even she laughed through her tears.

She, too, with the intermittent aid of artist friends, provided our early visual education. Baedeker was her Little Red Book and every summer we spent in Europe—England, France, Germany, Italy, Austria, Holland, or Switzerland depending on where work led them or they took us—Mother was the indefatigable guide. Churches, palaces, museums statues, fountains, tombs of the great—off we trudged staring our eyes out while Mother quoted and amplified Baedeker. There were times when Father and Leopold and I would have been happier sitting in a street café just gazing; and sometimes, when our guide succumbed, we did just that. Yet those summers—long before tourist hordes and cola signs—gave me feelings of beauty and heritage that I never forgot, greatly augmented by food I had never eaten, wines I was allowed to taste, and mountains there for the climbing.

In Pontresina, our favorite summer place, we climbed nearly every day: my parents above tree line, my brother and I much higher. From the age of twelve on nothing could keep me away from peaks. Roped together, rucksacks on back, we would follow a guide up and down precipitous rocks or dazzling glaciers. The rocks would frighten me more than the glaciers: the business of toeholds and fingerholds on vertical slabs between sky and abyss was tough, one slip and dangle terrifying. But I had to get to the top. I had to feel that incredible exaltation of being in a new and lonely dimension with the world spread below. Conquest? Yes, in a way. But more a sense of awesome majesty together with communion. With what? With that universal pattern, I guess. The intense clarity of the air at thirteen thousand feet is in itself an enlargement of being.

Coming down was worse than going up. It always is. But the vision of ascent was always dominant.

• • •

My brother tried to educate me in the basics of science. He would tell me why fire burned, why light refraction made your leg crooked in water, why stars seemed to twinkle, what the sun was made of, how to pitch a curve, and how sound traveled. He once said that if we could travel much, much faster than light, we could see Columbus landing. I didn't understand it then, and barely do now. But I believed everything he said and hoped, passionately, that it were true and that someday one could.

And then, when it was abundantly clear to him that I knew nothing at all about the basics of life, he tried to teach me something else.

He told me to come to his room, he wanted to show me something. I was about eleven then. Very solemnly, he took his penis out of his trousers and very solemnly, three paces away, I looked at it. I had never seen one before.

He told me to come closer and touch it. I did, very tentatively. He said not to be afraid, it wouldn't bite.

Actually, I didn't like the way it looked: a rather shabby assortment of shapes, I thought, and strangely colored. And crinkled. I was properly respectful, however, and probably said "Gee!" I don't think he told me what it was for; only that all boys had them.

One thing was sure, after this revelation. I had absolutely no desire, no desire at all, to have something like that swinging between my legs. It was much neater without it.

• • •

What's more, I couldn't square it with the only sex information, if you could call it that, imparted me by my mother. She told me that when a man and woman loved each other, the man planted a seed in the woman, which grew into a child. I couldn't quite figure how an object like Leopold's could plant anything, and even if it could, plant where?

I didn't know then that my mother hated to speak of "the facts of life" or, for that matter, bodily functions of any kind. In eighteen years she had told me only two things beyond the seed reference.

One, in answer to repeated pressing, was about birth. She said that my brother's birth was agonizingly painful; something about the size of his head and other complications; that mine was not quite as painful; and that in any case, it was worth all the suffering to have borne us. She said I would feel so too when the time came. She could not have known that this left me with a terror of childbirth that lasted for twenty more years.

So shy was my mother, in fact, about her body that she dressed and undressed under her nightgown. Much later she told me that she hated her body, so far it was from her conceptions of beauty. What this must have done to the marriage bed I never knew.

She did, to be sure, induct me gently when I was twelve or so into the reason and process of menstruation, which she assured me was nothing to be afraid of and part of being a woman. She was, it seemed, increasingly troubled by my delay in becoming one. At thirteen I was still flat as a board, all legs, with none of the budding graces of puberty; loathed dancing lessons designed to encourage them (the very "aesthetic" dance then in vogue, with gauzy scarfs and leaping with balloons); and refused ribbons in my underwear.

I was still a "tomboy" seething with new rebellions, questioning all conventions, and wanting to be something or someone that I was not.

Six years later I made this entry in a journal I kept that year:

The novel is hovering dangerously over the paper. Its theme will be that of the development of an imaginary girl through school, love, work, and death; her conception of each of these as opposed to the actuality. It sounds trite, but it assuredly will not be. May I summon the patience to carry it through.

I didn't. But the first part of this novel is—with the exception of altered names (I was "Jean Prell" and the professions of my parents professor-philosopher and singer) —straight reporting.

"O God, O God—(no, not God, I don't believe in God) O you, O anything, make me beautiful!"

When she was thirteen, dark-eyed, and lanky, she questioned God for the first time. It was in chapel at school while the girls were droning out the Lord's Prayer in a daze of early sleepiness.

"Are Father who art in Hea-ea-eaven, hallo-wed be thy nay-em"

Jean cautiously raised her head and looked around. Two hundred and ninety-nine bent heads mumbling about a mutual father. "Father"—that immediately implied a man; not a young man, but a fairly old man, for didn't he have hundreds of children? And didn't old man, especially if they were well known and dignified, wear beards? Suddenly Jean was disgusted. For six whole years she had bowed her head to a flesh and blood old man; imploring his grace in a dead, meaningless voice along with the other 299; every morning. She knew she didn't really mean a word of it.

"Mary," she said to her best friend at recess on the day of revelation. "Mary, I refuse to bow my head and say the Lord's Prayer ever again. I can't stand the hypocrisy."

"I stopped saying it a month ago!"

Jean felt a little flattened, but the excitement of a dangerous agreement outweighed her conceit, and she jumped on Mary's neck. This was friendship! She felt as if they were two brave medieval men defying the pope. And she wore a cynical smile on her face all morning, and talked very little. And when she told her parents what she had decided, her father beamed on her, overjoyed at the growth of wisdom. Her mother, too, was glad, but she neither smiled nor commented, being afraid of sponsoring heresy of any sort.

"Don't you see, dear," she said to her husband when they were alone, "if we praise her for every original thought she has, she'll think it smart to break away from everything, even the fine things of life."

Father shook his head slowly. "Don't worry about the kid. She's too sane to go to extremes. Anyway, thank God she's an individual! She doesn't need the crutches of the mass."

But she did. That night, lying on her bed, hemmed in by a speckled blackness that rang in her ears, she wanted to pray. She put her palms together and tried to conceive of a huge, formless Power, neither man, nor woman, nor animal. Then suddenly she put her hands down at her sides. "The gesture of praying is only for the old man I don't believe in any more. I mustn't use it. It's only a sort of Christian convention." But it was frightfully hard to keep the palms apart. They just had to come together, like magnets. It was the only way you could point at something. So she gave up the struggle and turned her mind to the next great question. What should she call the Power? *You* ________ that was the only possible name; direct, yet meaning nothing tangible or formal. "You—You—You, make me beautiful so the world will fall at my feet!"

She thought of her classmates undressing in the lockers before basketball. Their bones didn't show and their skins were radiantly white or smoothly olive, and their necks were set fairly on their shoulders. Hers hung out, like a camel's. Her skin was indeterminate, and shiny where it shouldn't be. Her knees were raw and jutted out. There were only three things she could pin her faith on: huge, somber gray eyes; a straight nose; and a neat, firm chin. Even at thirteen she thought, "If people only looked into my eyes, they would find me beautiful. They would forget everything else. There is something wonderful in my face—sometimes." But that wasn't enough. That was a sort of fraud, a sort of hypnotism. And so she prayed into the night for perfection.

• • •

Jean was unpopular with her contemporaries, and not yet quite magnetic enough for older friendships. The girls, except for the atheistic Mary and the sensitive Norma, disliked her with a suspicious dislike; for she had so many reserves, and they hated reserves. They hated anything they couldn't quite understand; and labeled it "conceit."

• • •

Jean read a theme one day all about a man who lost his soul one dark, howling night and rushed into the blackness to find it. Suddenly he saw it glimmering and shining through the shaking branches of a bare tree, and then again in the pond beneath the tree. And the pond being easier, he leaped in—and was drowned.

• • •

That evening after a discussion of educational desiccation, the whole family went to the symphony under Halter. They sat in a first-tier box because they knew the conductor well, and he loved to be able to smile at all the first-tier boxes when he bowed.

At that stage of her development, Jean was frankly more interested in the audience than in the music. She loved to sit in the dark red prominence and grin at her relatives across the horseshoe, and at all her mother's musical friends. And she loved to look down and study the complicated coiffures of homely, music-loving ladies.

And yet, the music affected her strongly. That night the orchestra played a Brahms symphony. Jean forgot the cousins across the way and the birds' nests beneath her. She stared wide-eyed and still at the orchestra, but saw no hectic violin bows, no brass, no kettledrums. She saw herself conquering the world. She saw herself riding out on a cloud above the heads of the people. More and more exalted she became, soaring inside. Glory! Glory! Glory! The child of God has come to us. Look, look, there she is gliding above us with a blinding light about her and divinity in her eyes. Brighter and brighter, breath-taking in the transfiguration of her face. And then the crucifixion. The blackness and the desolate roaring—*"Eli, Eli, lama sabachthani!"*

Jean felt drained of her blood and her eyes were hot and a little blurred, her throat tight. Then the music stopped, the clapping began.

Mother leaned over to Father.

"You can always trust Franz with Brahms."

"Halter," of course, was Damrosch, "Franz" was Walter —the star of the family, my magnetic uncle.

"Don't people like you?"

"No—only about two girls and one teacher. The principals and the other teachers can't stand me."

"But why? Aren't you very good in your studies? I always thought you were the model schoolgirl."

Jean smiled—wryly, and looked down.

"Well, I guess that's the trouble. They say they like good, conscientious girls, but they really don't. They like the silly, pretty girls. They're less trouble."

"Less trouble?"

"Yes—. They smile a lot and never think much and don't have funny ideas. And principals and teachers hate me because I know more than they do. They say I look sullen. They think just because I'm thirteen I don't know anything. And half the time they're so stupid they don't understand what I'm saying. Damn them!"

• • •

Jean at fifteen was not much different from Jean at thirteen. Her neck was perhaps a little shorter, her knees a little less obtrusive. But she still looked like a tragic muse; still laughed at things one shouldn't laugh at; still rebelled; and still had an imagination that gave her agony and joy surpassing agony . . .

• • •

Food was really the first step in Jean's discovery of her physical self. It was one of the few things about which she had no inhibitions. She reveled in good food; and only remained thin because her mental and emotional intensity consumed it as soon as it was swallowed. The smell of hot fudge or burnt almonds or buttered asparagus would drive her almost crazy with delight; and she could scarcely eat for excitement. Many people thought it disgusting and called her greedy; and she knew it.

"It's much more disgusting," she would retort, "to take a tiny sliver of chicken when you'd give your soul for the whole wing." Hypocrisy of any sort pained her deeply.

Now, when she was getting on in her fifteenth year, a new sense awoke. She realized that her body was an inferior sort of thing, but heretofore had done nothing actual about it. She had prayed; but had refused to dance. So she conceived of making herself beautiful in a new, secret way; secret so that no one would tease her about it. When she went to bed at night she put two pillows under her back and none under her head, and stayed in this arched position until her stomach muscles felt as if they would never snap back. She had a vague idea that this would put everything into shape. Besides that, she would direct her thoughts to every portion of herself in turn. To her arms she would say, "You've got to grow muscles, you've got to grow muscles, you've got to get brawny"; to her neck, "You've got to get thick, you've got to get round, you've got to get shorter"; to her shoulder blades and collarbones, "Disappear, get out of sight, sink in, disappear." And so on. This she kept up for nearly a month, at the end of which she could find no improvement. Dampened but firm, she kept at herself, not with regular formulas and back-archers, but with a powerful imagination. Instead of desiring to be this and that, she pretended she was this and that.

In the "novel," this pretense reached a climax in a scene, again true, in which "Norma," my best friend, and I acted out fantasies induced by a common passion for Rider Haggard.

She and I had the run of her apartment one afternoon, and I suggested that she dress up like a sort of White Goddess, veils and all, and that I would be a visiting king from an alien shore. She should dance for me, I would be overcome by passion. But the curse was that anyone who kissed her would fall dead.

What happened then would later, no doubt, have been

construed as a Lesbian orgy, although we never touched each other except for that fatal and fleeting embrace, after which I immediately crumpled to the floor and twitched my way into death.

Before that we provided musical accompaniment by putting a record of *Le Coq d'Or* on the victrola, and danced to it in the best Diaghilev manner. During the course of this, her veils kept falling off and I saw her for the first time without any clothes.

I was so struck with the beauty of her body that after my "death" I took off my clothes too and danced a solo to the same record.

"Something was being born in her," I wrote five years later, "and she knew it. A worship, and adoration of self, of the powers of self. She knew she was long and white and moved in perfect ways. She felt the litheness of her thighs and the wiry control of her torso, and the arching of her neck. And music poured ecstasy into her, and her into ecstasy."

My friend and I concocted other legends and danced them out to music. We were innocent beyond belief. This was the only way—in that far, stifled day—that we could accept our bodies and rejoice in them. Secretly, because nobody else would understand.

• • •

This propriety was not only the temper of the time but of our school. Miss Veltin, our French principal, managed to couch it in the grace of her language, which we had to speak exclusively not only during French classes but between all others and even in recess. But our American headmistress, whose distinguished descendants I will spare by calling her

"Miss Jenks," her novel name, exuded propriety from every hated pore.

We feared and loathed her.

Miss Jenks was a well-padded upright woman in the early fifties. She always wore net guimpes with high collars, and her hair cleverly rolled up from her face and neck. A bird's-eye view would look like a thick pewter pot cover with a knob in the center. The knob was the knot. The girls were sure the roll was hollow and used as a sort of mouse runway. She invariably wore some childish little bead necklace, usually blue, picked up in solitary European wanderings. A strange mixture of granite and coquetry, Miss Jenks. Her eyes were a glacier blue, set shallowly under disappearing wispy eyebrows. Disappearing because, at the slightest disapproval, they would vanish up in the roll. Her nose was straight but pinched; her lips straighter and more pinched. But sometimes her eyes would look filmy and her mouth soften at the corners. When a particularly meritorious class graduated, for instance, or a speech was made in her honor. It was a formality to have everything planned by the student body passed under her nose for censorship. She adored the prerogative.

Aware of this, a committee from our class had approached her with some plans for a school entertainment which, to our rage, she turned down. After she had dismissed us with "Good morning" I describe a recurrent fantasy as follows:

Jean, pale with fury, rushed up and slapped her in the face. "Damn you, you spirit-crusher, you oppressor of youth, damn you! You're killing us with your hardness and cruelty, you're draining the life out of us. You don't understand. You don't know what beauty is, or youth, or fire. Damn you and your icy eyes and iron mouth. You're a murderess, that's what you are, a slayer of the spirit . . . !"

Then the picture changed suddenly to the assembly room with the whole school seated in it, silently, Miss Jenks at her imperial desk in the imperial platform at the head of the aisle.

The principal, her roll more regular than ever, her neck more upright, said, "Will Jean Prell please step up on the platform?"

Jean did so, very white and quiet.

"Do you see this girl?" asked Miss Jenks of the school, "Well, she did this and that and so on," explaining what had happened. And when the story was finished, she gave Jean a terrible blow in the face, which left a livid patch on her drained cheek. Then she began to tear her clothes from her, right there in front of the school. Jean said not a thing, but stood there with her clothes falling in tatters about her, her feet bare, her skin bruised. And the school laughed. And laughed and laughed. Until, suddenly, a strange shaft of light struck Jean diagonally and wrapped her in a golden haze. And she lifted up her agonized face into the radiance and was calmed. And an awful silence fell upon the school. Then she dropped in a faint on the platform.

The martyr rode again.

But there were compensations at Veltin. Doubly, since I might have been languishing in another school called St. Agnes on West Eighty-seventh Street off Broadway.

I was taken there for my first day of school by my nurse. After she left, I took one look around, met my teacher, sat in a class, excused myself, and fled. I ran all the way down Broadway and across to my home, crying.

My mother opened the door and I flew in her arms. When she asked me why, and what had happened (she told me later), I bawled and quavered, "It's like a church, and I hate the faces!" and "it's so *far!*"

She knew well enough, poor woman, that neither firmness nor gentle persuasion would get me back there. So, because of parental charm and cultural distinction, Veltin took me in on a scholarship and there I stayed: one block away, and on the whole, not unhappily. My natural passion for learning was met by two teachers, especially, with a natural passion for teaching: Miss Sweet in English, and Madame Carrière in French.

Miss Sweet taught me the structure of English, the meaning of words, and the beauty of great writing in verse and prose and drama. Madame Carrière took me from Villon and Voltaire to Molière and Racine to de Musset and Baudelaire and Verlaine to Victor Hugo and Zola and Balzac, among many others. We had to write our essays in French, memorize and intone yards of mournful and noble Alexandrians with the right inflections, translate poems into English, and write our own in French.

From a tall and rather gloomy teacher we had four years of Latin in which we had not only to translate from Caesar and Cicero and others, but write our own puny wars in their language. In the last years we were given a play called *Ulysses* to perform, in Latin, of course, before an audience of school and parents.

A young stock-company director was brought in to pull

us together, map out our movement and, finally, put on our make-up.

On Ulysses (me) he pasted a lush and tawny beard to match my hair, and the effect so ravished our teacher that she kept stroking it and me, noting a marked resemblance, she said, to Christ. This disturbed me a little, but I strode on stage and did the best I could until the climactic moment when I was to kill my wife's suitors with a bow and arrow.

I was expressly urged to fake this act: that is, aim for the curtained door stage left, draw back the bow, then let the arrow fall. In the tension of the moment, however, I followed through. The arrow whizzed through the opening, followed instantaneously by a muffled shriek: that of the teacher missed by a feathered inch.

Homicidal or not, bored as I often was, I was glad for that Latin, believing it gave me a sense of word and structure that not only made Italian and French far easier to learn, but encouraged precision in language if not in thought.

In all these courses (now doomed, I suppose, by "irrelevance") I averaged consistent nineties through the years, not through superior intellect but out of sheer hunger. Madame Carrière, in fact, repeatedly and salubriously told me that I was not brilliant; merely intelligent. Of my capacity for a sensible life, moreover, she had grave doubts. Shaking her floppy pompadour at some flaming opinions, gratuitously voiced, she would say *"Ma pauvre fille, tu va marier une tête de negre, sois sûr!"*

In those days "marrying some black fellow" meant, simply, being a fool.

• • •

To most of the girls, however, I was a stuck-up prig. Class president time after time, those high marks (except in math), that straight hair and serious face; hand always raised. Clever, yes, but who did she think she was? My only real friends, an ebullient atheist and the sensitive "Norma" knew. Under my name in the school yearbook of the senior class, the former quoted Alexander Pope: "Chaos of thought and passion, all confused"; and followed him with these comments:

The ego, of course, must play its large part in any life, but in some, we think, it looms larger than in others. Now M. although—or perhaps because—she has her due proportion of egoism, manifests a blundering desire for sincerity and truthful expression in all matters. There also bristle from her even more intolerance than is necessary for positiveness, a preference for nearly all innovations, particularly intellectual innovations of the 20th century over those of any other period, and a peevish genius in art. She is a shining light in fencing with foils and sarcastic words of fifty syllables.

I wished she had added that for one year I was captain of the basketball team, won a game, and in the roars of my classmates was, for the first time, accepted; maybe forgiven.

• • •

Nobody knew, however, that I took (and still do) the *mens sana in corpore sano* bit very seriously. Not through group sports, which I never really liked, but through making my body a tensile and variable instrument.

I still had my trapeze at home, and in the school gym I was an acknowledged whiz on rings and bars.

But in privacy I practiced a number of arcane experiments with my physical self. I managed at one time to make myself faint at will. I deliberately ordered my blood to drain from my brain and my consciousness to recede until grayness overtook me—and scared me stiff. I decided to leave that be.

But another experiment was very pleasing. I had noticed in summer how horses, afflicted with flies, would twitch them off wherever they settled just by moving a specific area of skin or muscle. So starting with my scalp and ears I managed to twitch off imaginary flies settling all the way down my body without moving anything except the tickled spot. This skill proved more satisfying than useful.

One summer, the family went en masse to the Folies-Bergère in Paris. During the intermission I wandered around to see the various side shows in the lobby, transfixed by one. She was a belly dancer, and I vowed I would never be happy until I mastered her astounding gyrations.

I did master them, again in private. But as time went on, I could not bear to hide this splendid talent, embarrassing what friends I did not amuse by displaying it freely at parties. Much later I had to curb this public display on behalf of nervous husbands. But on the whole it had its uses, and even now—in a series of exercises dreamed up for the preservation of the flesh—it helps. Long life to belly dancers.

• • •

Yet even before these mindless pursuits, the pleasures of scholarship had begun to wane.

They shut you up from eight-thirty to one-thirty every morning for ten years. And every day they cram five different subjects into you. And each teacher says sweetly, "All I ask of you, girls, is one hour of homework. Surely you can do that," entirely forgetting that four other teachers say the same thing.

Thus Jean would "groan to her parents."

Yet she had little cause to complain compared to the other victims. . . . Preparation with her was the grasping of salient facts which her imagination could embroider in class. She would skim over ninety lines of Virgil, see the words "Aeneas," "Dido," "cave," "thunderstorm," and shut the book for the night. That was all she needed.

"It isn't that I work so frightfully hard," she would explain, "but that it's all such useless stuff; and that it takes a quarter of your life to learn it."

These mounting reactions were given callow form in the class play I wrote in my senior year, called *Utopia*. It was set in the age of Pericles, at the Academy at Athens, Greece. I was, of course, Plato.

Plato: Aristotle, what have you observed lately of life and of those who enjoy it?

Aristotle: I have observed, master, that those who educate the young question *them* but never question themselves.

Plato: An excellent, though somewhat irreverent observation. Why do you think this is so, Aristotle?

Aristotle: It is so, master, because usually only those instruct who think they have found the answers to nearly everything, and, having found them, consider their searching over, and become as static as the stars in the sky.

• • •

Hippocrates: Master, I think this woman Sappho is an outrage! She is representative of this dangerous feminist movement now springing up! Fancy a woman writing poetry!

Plato: And why shouldn't a woman write poetry?

Hippocrates: Women were created merely to further the race of men.

Plato: You ignorant young cub! The only charge against the female sex is that one of them bore you!

The play drew mixed reviews, especially from Miss Jenks. She would have her revenge before long.

In the meantime I was writing papers for Miss Sweet that ranged from a defense of the length of Dickens and a review of Shaw's *Cashel Byron's Profession* (unfavorable) to a study of the decline of Rome called "Society in Transition: 4th and 5th Centuries A.D." On this paper (my parents never threw away anything their children did), now yellow and tattered from decades of storage, is written

---

H.C. (high credit): Very interesting paper well thought out, a contribution":

one of Miss Sweet's rare accolades.

I was also writing unsolicited French verse of a sentimentality so mawkish that Madame Carrière must have had a hard time reacting with a straight face to lines like this from a pale string bean of sixteen:

O Dieu impuissant! Ciel cruel et sourd!
D'une pauvre âme tu n'entends pas les cris?
Ah, d'infinies larmes mon corps las est lourd . . .
Rends-moi mon fils, je te dis!

After a few sobbing refrains of

> Le printemps vient, mais mon beau garçon pas—
> Les fleurs sont ouvertes, mais il n'est point là!

I closed on a wave of anguish:

> Et voilà la plainte que j'entends dans le noir,
> Q'une femme sanglote et chante
> Dans une voix toute pleine de désespoir,
> La voix d'une suppliante.

Since I had no "beau garçon" and was by no means a "femme," it was as phony as a three-dollar bill: the result clearly, of too much reading and too little living.

My mother, a pool of sentiment behind her Roman façade, was easily moved: a patsy, in fact. I therefore showered my parents regularly with verse at birthdays, anniversaries, and at Christmas, using one occasion to express in hand-illuminated text, my deep distrust and aversion to formal religion. It was called *Venite, Exultemus Domino!—A Poem Typifying the Spirit of the Religious Christmas.* It concerned a procession of "cowlèd monks" celebrating that day, and each line was followed by the Latin incantation above. A sample will suffice:

Their long, thin hands were humbly crossed upon their suffering chests—

(V.E.D.!)

God save all those poor sinners with their laughs and idle jests,

(V.E.D.!)

And bless all those who live a life of prayer and
supplication,
(V.E.D.!)
And sacrifice their very flesh for pious concentration.
(V.E.D.!)
The fearsome line of chanting monks passed slowly
through the night
(V.E.D.!)
O God! was this the birthday of Christ, the everlasting
light?
(V.E.D.)

At fifteen, "Chaos of thought and passion, all confused." A fundamental religiosity, in the sense of a faith in some intangible greatness both in and beyond human experience, a love for Christ warring angrily with repressive dogma and ritual. A craving for knowledge being slowly superseded by a craving for sensation.

The following half of a poem also dedicated to my mother somewhat later is evidence enough: It was called *Lament for Primitive Simplicity and Power*—Greek form.

Woe I cry for the Senses, and the loves cry woe again—
Where is the strength of biting teeth,
Where is the cleanness of the sheath of the spirit?
Where is the nostril's keenness, where the ear
Attuned to noiseless voices, soundless sounds?
Oh tell me where
The eye aware of the colors in grayness, the sweep of the
wind through space,
Where are the sensing lips, and where those hands
Feeling the shadows . . . the volume of a curve?

Where . . . where?
Woe I cry for the Senses, and the loves cry woe again.

In the same batch for her were translations of poems by Baudelaire (of course inadequate, if not shameful) and of Gerhart Hauptmann.

My only audience for these attempts was family. We knew musicians and artists but in those years no writers to speak of. I am sometimes tempted to wonder whether early direction and encouragement by a good poet could not have made me one too. But honesty compels a truer reason. The vow of spiritual chastity and material abnegation essential, I think, to the real poet, I could not take. Because I could not deny myself anything, I denied my self.

• • •

My last years at school I was straining on the leash. Sick of routine but working doubly hard, yearning for freedom and change. I was growing taller and taller, increasingly conscious not only of height but of how I looked to others. Still totally ignorant of sex, I was amazed and pleased when older men called me beautiful, but when I looked at snapshots of myself in dragging skirts I wondered whether I would ever be desired.

My brother wondered too. We were very close but his natural affection was countered by a very real fear for my future. Rational, brilliant, organized, cautious, controlled, he watched my headlong lurch into life with as much dismay as amusement. He knew me to be without guile, sense, or the instinct for self-preservation. Sometimes he told me so, sometimes he hoped to rein me in by deflation.

One day he looked at me dressed to go out in some shapeless garment with a beret slapped on my head, and he shook his own. "I just can't imagine," he said grinning, "how any man would ever want to marry you!"

I couldn't either.

But marriage was never on my mind those days; only romantic love. That was still in books and music and in the way some men looked at me and I looked at them while a mysterious heat started to spread; and a nameless longing.

• • •

(Handwritten fragment . . . of what? Doubtless another aborted "novel," with changed names. Probably age fifteen.)

James Burton
Attorney-at-Law
Boston

Dear Mrs. Wodenhaus,

I cannot resist the temptation of telling what a delightful evening I had at your house the other night.

It was a privilege to be included, even for a moment in the intimacy of your home—a home of rare beauty and civilization.

The food was a revelation, the talk stimulating, and your singing balm to the ear. May I add, too, that you have an extraordinary daughter? I shall watch her career with interest.

Gratefully,
James Burton

• • •

Dear Mr. Burton,

You probably won't recognize who I am. I am Harold Wodenhaus' daughter—tall and queer-looking.

Now that that's settled, I want to thank you for what

you said in your letter to Mother. She didn't want me to see but Father grabbed it away from her and showed it to me.

Those kind words have dragged me from the depths of despair. I was almost going to give up. People think I'm peculiar and I amuse them but you're about the first to see anything attractive about me, and you don't know what it means.

Anyway I think you are the perfect type of a gentleman. There aren't many left. As for boys of my own age, I despise them. They haven't a single idea in their beans —or anywhere!

Hoping to see you again someday and go on talking, I remain,

Very sincerely yours,
Nora Wodenhaus

• • •

James Burton
Attorney-at-Law
Boston

My dear Miss Wodenhaus,

I shall be in New York on business during the coming week. ~~Will you do me the honor of~~ [sic] Will you have a bus ride with me on Wednesday afternoon, and further settle the affairs of the world?

If you are able to extend me this privilege, telephone me at the Chatham Hotel on Monday, at about five o'clock.

Hopefully,
James Burton

• • •

(Written by "Nora," apparently after extending above privilege: M.M.)

He looked me in the eye for a long time and then said, in a low voice, "Nora, you will be very beautiful someday." I nearly expired. Imagine!

He's practically the only man I've ever met outside of Father who had any sense. Not about my looks, of course —I mean generally. ~~I don't know see how I can live without —————— until I see him again~~ [sic]

The awful thing about it is that he lives in Boston most of the time. Oh My God—

• • •

James Burton
Attorney-at-Law
Boston

Dear Harold,

Do you mind if I have designs on your daughter? She's amazing.

As ever,
Jim

P.S. Purely paternal, of course.

• • •

My dear Jim,

Go ahead only don't tell my wife.

I don't give a damn what you do the kid. I can't imagine a better beginning for her.

As ever,
Harold

• • •

While I was conjuring up Mr. Burton, the perfect gentleman, I was also, it now appears, concerning myself with far more tangible images.

The evidence consists of four pages of penciled writing, suggesting my fifteenth or sixteenth year, on the lined school paper used for required themes.

This one was titled "Photography" and traced the history

of its birth and development with a factual detail and technical grasp quite foreign to my usual easy flamboyance.

Near the end and after the mention and explanation of the three forms of color photography—direct, additive, and subtractive—four lines are scratched out and a note in my brother Leopold's handwriting scribbled in the margin, so abbreviated as to be, for me, barely decipherable. My own writing then emerges again with

> And finally, in the two color-subtractive process, we find the well-known Prizma, Colura, Cinechrome, and the Mannes-Godowsky process, which is the highest point reached in the development of color photography, because of its great simplicity.

Then (in L's handwriting):

> A single exposure is made on a plate or film in an ordinary camera. Moreover any number of positives may be printed from the same plate as desired—a virtue which makes the process as easy to manipulate as plain black and white photography.

Two things could explain this collaboration of his mind and my pencil. One, that being the only person in school with this information, I chose to flaunt the monopoly in class. Two, that Leopold dictated it to me for his own use during these last school years when I served as the first secretary to the two young inventors of Kodachrome: both musicians, both sons of musicians, Leo's father being the famous pianist Leopold Godowsky.

Germinating when they were both seventeen at the Riverdale School, carried on through college years, and then developed in a primitive "laboratory" in a Broadway hotel, their experiments were bearing first fruits and already attracting Wall Street and Eastman attention.

Since they had no money then except family contributions that barely covered the rent and essential equipment, the typewriter skills I had taught myself were, to my great delight, solicited. I would trot to their hotel lair after school in the afternoons, take down in longhand letters, statements, and incomprehensible formulae, then go home to type them up for later signing.

I also doubled as model. On winter days I posed on the roof of our apartment house in extraordinary assortments of colors while the boys snapped and snapped. I was naturally thrilled to be part of the project, and even more thrilled when—in the garage "lab" of a rented summer cottage—we saw the first films in color: haloed, overintense, not always true, but—color. Me in blue, red, green, with greenish or orange skin, but—me. Part of something important, part of the life of extraordinary young men to whom, for once, I was not a drag or a nuisance.

I was also, as Leopold well knew, a perfect target for kidding. I believed everything anybody said to me. I would swallow the most outrageous statements hook, line and sinker.

One afternoon when I reported to the lab at the Alamac, the boys greeted me with special effusion and told me that they had discovered something new and truly sensational. I would be the first to know it and see it. It had taken them weeks, they said, possibly years, but here it was at last.

They hustled me into the darkroom and with great ceremony Leopold lifted a vial containing something cloudy—

liquid or vapor. They told me to come close. I did. I smelt something extremely noxious, and asked what it was.

"We have," said Leo, "managed finally to reproduce in synthetic form the human belch."

Manic laughter followed my exit.

3.

Finally the whole school, except the finished products, sat. The organist pushed in and pulled out a lot of stops, slid up and down the bench, looking feverishly into the mirror that reflected the aisle and the doings of the school, changed gear, and drowned the air with a slow, masterful march designed for the entrance of the graduating class.

They came—the halt, the lame, and the blind. Halt with weakness, lame with fear, blind with emotion. Some kept their balance on the ground and their heads in the air, conscious of the impression they were making. Some were too miserable with nervousness to make an effect. And all of those who swore they would not be unseated and sentimentalized by the mere process of graduating swallowed hard and felt the end had come. Down they came, two by two, burdened with roses and eighteen years of ignorance; tall, beautiful, short, golden, dumpy;

fresh, voluptuous, curly-haired, sallow, straight-haired; stupid, average, intelligent; healthy—introspective. But white, white, white—and exalted, holy. Now the eyes of the mothers of the graduates filled. And the eyes of Miss Jenks watered—the sad smile returning—rainbow—.

Ah, Miss Jenks—in a peacock-blue gown draped in the fashion of the Greeks she so adored, with a peacock-blue necklace about her guimpe and peacock-blue combs in her pewter pot-cover—swept stiffly yet humbly down the aisle to her dais. Then the processional—"Ane-shunt of days . . ."

Thus the five-year-older ghost, describing, presumably, the last commencement ceremonies before her own.

When the parchments had been distributed and partial silence established, a tall, dark, assured girl with intelligent Jewish features rose from the honored class onto the platform and bowed. She was the valedictorian—"the girl of highest standing in character and work." Jean knew her only slightly, but admired her immensely. She had a bold, original mind and great sensitiveness.

"As we leave this dear scene of childhood and childhood dreams, like little ships sailing from the quiet harbor into the stormy seas of life . . ."

Dismayed, Jean wondered what had happened. "Little ships—stormy sea of life." Not Judith, certainly not Judith! How could she? Why, those foolish little ships sailed out every single year. The marine simile was the joke of the school. And Judith, bold, brilliant Judith, had said what a score of girls had said before her. Oh—oh—oh! How awful. "My God, wait till I get there, I'll give 'em a shock. Little ships nothing! Battleships! Men-o'-

war! Cruisers! Going out of the harbor to smash up every damn thing in sight. Shoot, blow up, ram, race. To hell with the stormy sea! Weaklings!" She had rushed up on the platform and was exhorting the school to spiritual war. "You pitiful children, you spineless babes afraid to get caught in the whirlwind—!"

The clergyman resumed his seat. The movement brought Jean down to earth and made her wonder what she had missed. The Benediction probably. It didn't matter. Inarticulate benignity.

The organist went vigorously into action, the school rose and walked out to an ominous French military march. Miss Jenks had French blood. Her mother was a Trevizant.

"Judith," of course, was myself. Because of the infamy of my own disgrace at my own graduation, I could not—*could* not—attribute it to "Jean."

I now can.

When I was elected valedictorian of my class, I was determined to change the old, stale, pattern. I asked Miss Jenks whether I could write the valedictory in verse.

She said, "Well, we have never done it before, and I'm sure Mademoiselle Veltin would agree that prose is traditional and suitable."

I stood there, my hands behind my back, and finally said: "But, Miss Jenks, I have already written it in verse!" and bringing my arms forward, I slowly placed the pages on her polished desk.

Miss Jenks glanced at them briefly and with a thin smile said: "I shall read it and discuss it with Miss Veltin."

"My dear," said Miss Veltin kindly the next day, "we are

not very happy with it as it is. . . . certain passages seem unsuitable . . . and then—the verse . . ."

Subdued but still resisting I wrote a second and then a third draft, determined—in the face of all omens—to speak in verse.

The portions of each that follow are not offered here—God knows—as indications of poetic talent but as ludicrous or pathetic evidence of what was to be a hopeless effort to temper their objections without sacrificing my intent: to contain a seething rebellion in the lofty rhetoric and iambic pentameter appropriate, I assumed, to the occasion. We were not then allowed the luxury of the raised fist and the shouted insult.

Valedictory

There is a momentary emptiness
That frightens us; the lull, the quietude
Preceding birth—for we are being born
From childhood's irresponsibility
Into maturity——
—and now for the first time
Straining in the eternal fight of man
To break some prison walls . . .

Valedictory

At last the great transition has arrived
Now every minute we are changing, growing,
Stirring within and now for the first time,
Straining in the eternal fight of man
To burst his prison walls, for even here . . .

Valedictory

Forbear with us if we seem pale and hushed,
Wide-eyed and tremulous this radiant morn;

Wonder and apprehension make us so,
For soon the great awakening will come,
Toward which we have been growing all these years
With eager vision. . . .

When all three were turned down, outrage flooded my soul. I told my headmistresses I would speak as I wanted and not as they asked, I wailed my fury to my long-suffering parents, and Miss Jenks asked to see them after Father had tried by phone to negotiate a settlement. They went to her office.

Later that evening, they reported that Miss Jenks had said, "Your daughter will be broken on the wheels of life!" They thought this was more funny than I did, and pled with me for once to be a little more temperate, to understand others. They said why spoil the last days of a splendid school career? They said, after you leave, you can say anything you want in any way you want, but traditions are traditions, like them or not, these ladies are growing old and a little set.

Relax, Leopold said; grinning of course.

That was the last thing I did. On the dining room table that night, alone I wrote—with a furious perversity—a parody of all the valedictorian clichés I had suffered for ten years. To spare you, I offer only a few of the shameful lines:

Courage! You who are straining to go forward, to burst these walls of sheltered serenity! Fear nothing, not the battering of Fate, not the blind opposition of old spirits who would crush out your brave illusions. [Had to work that one in! M.M.] . . .

Welcome exultantly the turbulence into which you are soon to be whirled, crave unceasingly the beauty and the glory of life. . . . Therefore, courage!

As a final gesture of abject appeasement I quoted Henley's "It matters not how strait the gate,/How charged with punishments the scroll,/I am the master of my fate;/I am the captain of my soul."

Not bloody likely: I had sold it up the river. Here was this girl, already five feet ten and a half inches tall, thin pillar in white, skin yellow from recent jaundice, hand holding the single American beauty rose, intoning garbage.

Here was the *magna cum laude* diploma (honors in French), fencer, bugler, rebel, searcher for truth—talking (what I can only now call) crap.

And which—to stand as a solemn reminder of treachery-on-high and treason to self—I stuck away in a box, now feeling secure enough (only just) to confess the crime.

• • •

By then, the results of my college entrance exams had come in, with such a high percentile that letters arrived from three of the leading eastern colleges inviting me as a student—if needed, on scholarship.

My parents were happy and impressed. I was pleased by the marks, but disturbed by the letters. When they asked me which of these colleges I would choose, I said: none. I told them I didn't want to go to college.

Astounded, disappointed, they naturally asked my why: It was a wonderful privilege, I had earned it, they were not only ready but eager to give me one thousand dollars toward the tuition, matched by a thousand which my Mannes grandparents—who could ill afford it—had saved up all these years for Leopold and for me.

I was touched but determined. The reason, I told them, why I didn't want to go to college was that I could not endure another four years with girls, that I didn't want to learn from books any more. I wanted to live. Perhaps because I said this quietly, with no emotional burst, none of the usual defiance, they argued no further. Remarkable people that they were, they said: it is your life, you must live it, we only can pray that you are doing the right thing.

To this day I don't know whether I did or not. But I am reasonably sure that my alternative course—a year away from home—taught me things I would never have learned in a girls' college and in those days.

• • •

Four months passed, however, before this break. The trauma of graduation was followed by a summer of swimming and gaiety on eastern Long Island and then by a move to the East Side long desired by my parents since they founded their music school, six years before, on East Seventy-fourth Street. They had postponed the move, commuting daily across the Park, because of my stubborn insistence that my only friends were at my school.

The new apartment was on Seventy-fifth Street, between Park and Lexington. The indispensable Tante lived there with us, and Leopold had a small adjoining flat with a separate entrance.

The golden oak was jettisoned at last, but thanks to Mother the same general atmosphere prevailed: of light and peace and pleasure to the eye.

Once installed, my mother felt that I should "come out."

I flinched at the thought even though she envisaged a very modest affair, and finally said that I would "leak out."

The date was set, the day came. I had prepared a very odd costume for it. I had dyed my white graduation dress, full of fringes, red, and fashioned a sort of wreath of shiny black grapes to put on my head. My parents swallowed, looked at each other, and decided on silence. This was clearly no time for a typical rendition of the Tragic Muse.

The guests were mostly older friends of my parents whom I both liked and respected in spite of their conventional mode and the furry chins of some of the wives. (Women of a certain age never pulled out their whiskers then.) There were a few musicians, and very few people under thirty. I dimly remember one unhappy WASP young man who looked about him as if he were in Afghanistan and viewed me with an indifference tinged with alarm.

The food was lovely, everybody was very nice, but Mother conceded that the hoped-for admirers of her daughter were not in evidence. She then, poor dear, so strong and so innocent, decided that weekly At-Homes might draw them to my side, and sent out cards to the effect that Mrs. and Miss Mannes would be receiving for tea every Thursday from four until six.

It was a disaster even without grapes. For two consecutive Thursdays we sat there, my mother and I, chatting without conviction or joy while no doorbell rang.

On the third it finally did, sounding the arrival of a son of some Baltimore friends. He was tall and stalwart, black of hair and hot of eye, polite, and easy with small talk. My mother, radiant with relief, stayed a short while, then excused herself and left me to my fate.

My fate had little to say, and I'm afraid I tried to keep

things going by talking of sonnets or plays, which were not his bag. Sports at Yale were certainly not mine.

He nobly asked me to dinner, nevertheless, and after a little food and wine animation set in. I used a few *femme-fatale* tricks I had seen in movies, narrowing my eyes and looking deep into his, fingering my long fake pearls and laughing at nothing.

They worked all too well. In a taxi, ostensibly on my way home, he struck with full force. Lips hard on mine, hand down my dress, heaving and panting, tongue in ear, the works. At least, the first works ever practiced upon me. I was both hot and terrified. I didn't know it came so fast, without any words, without tenderness, or music, or love.

Frantic, I pushed him away from me with all my force, saying no, please, no, Please, No!

He finally sat back, running his fingers through his flopping hair, still breathing hard.

"I suppose you want to go home," he said.

I nodded.

We rode in silence while I adjusted my dress.

As we drew to the door of my apartment house, he said in a low voice, "Faker! Next time a fellow takes you out—if he ever does—don't look at him that way if you don't mean it!"

Mother was upstairs waiting. I went past her to my room without looking or speaking, closed the door, and threw myself choking with sobs on my bed. No role, for once.

• • •

The next day he called to apologize. He even asked me out. I thanked him and said it was my fault and I was sorry, but I couldn't go.

I was too ashamed of my ignorance to find out what he wanted to do with me—or to me.

• • •

The plans for my year abroad had been clear in my mind from the start, and clearly conveyed.

I wanted to go to England. What I had seen of it on family trips had delighted me. What I had read of it, from King Arthur and his knights through Conan Doyle's *Sherlock Holmes* (an addiction of Father and brother) impelled me there. From the Round Table to Baker Street, England was my region of dreams and longing.

I wanted to study sculpture during that year. Not because London was a center of art: I didn't have to be told that the heart of painting and sculpture was in Paris. But because I felt a great need to follow my second urge for expression: visual and tactile rather than thought and print.

From the age of ten I had always played with form: plasteline, wood, then clay. I was obsessed with the human and animal body, the human face. My notebooks were full of drawings, wherever I was: of musicians playing, of strangers in trains, of dancers and bullfighters.

In the summer of my sixteenth year our family, together with one of my closest friends from school (the atheist), spent several weeks in the high Pyrenees at a remote village. Staying there with us by plan were close friends: Professor Robert W. Wood and Mrs. Wood. Professor Wood was one of the great physicists of his time, especially in the field of optics and light. This made him not only a superb mentor and confidant for Leopold and the developing process of color photography, but the Johns Hopkins sage was also an ardent amateur painter.

Like a number of men much older than myself, he liked

to be with me. We trudged together into the mountains, paint box in hand, agreed on a fortuitous spot, and went to work. What we produced (at least *these* were not kept) remain in my memory as a series of small chromos, of which very few—either his or mine—we could be proud. But we loved the doing of them, we learned from each other, and for me the glory of being treated as a friend and painting colleague of this great scientist infused my being.

Others equally respectful of his mind, however, would deplore his jokes ("bad taste") which Father and Leopold relished; and once someone said it was too bad he was such a lecher. I knew the word from Ben Jonson and other Restoration sources, but not its full meaning. (I thought it meant "roisterer" or something like that.) Certainly, he patted my shoulder and often gazed at me intently, but it wasn't until the next year or so that I began to get the point. At his summer home, an old barn in East Hampton, he had a powerful telescope mounted on a stand and approached by a flight of wooden steps. I was looking one night with awe at the conical icecaps, or poles, of Mars when I felt his hand lightly stroking my thighs and buttocks. It was distracting but pleasant, and although at last I assumed that this was lechery, I thoroughly liked it. Was it not, after all, a sign of affection from a good old friend? (And one, incidentally, who remained so as long as he lived.)

Painting, however, was not for me. Although in life color played a vital part, on paper or canvas line was preeminent. And then line was not enough. I craved three dimensions, I wanted to feel with my hands what I saw with my eyes.

There was for me no physical pleasure attached to typing or even to drawing now. The senses began to take over.

Hence sculpture was large in the plans for a release which

I sorely needed. Release from a society which I knew would try to force me into a woman's mold I did not want—marriage, children, domestic absorption. Release from surveillance, loving or critical. Release, in short, from the familiar, the safe, the expected. Release, more than anything, and with real pain, from a family nest so warm, so complete in itself, and so cherished that I might never break free without this deliberate flight.

And one thing more. I was in love with Englishmen. At eight I was enamored of Sir Gawain, and it never stopped. Walking the streets of London in adolescent summers, I thought I had never seen such beautiful men in my life. The clean bones of their faces, the freshness of skin, the burnished thickness of their hair, the impeccable limbs in impeccable clothes. How different these were from the brilliant polyglot men in our living room!

My parents, even my father, conceded this too. He, because he had a natural elegance and love of aristocratic bearing (those actors in the Union Square Theatre); mother because she was by nature (and after one glass of wine or schnapps) a flirtatious soul. She knew that she frightened men with her exacting intelligence, but she melted before any man perceptive enough to brush it aside and address her as woman. The voices of Englishmen melted her even more.

This shared affection for English life and ways helped to soften, if not blunt, their deeper concern about my launch into space. It was a brave and tortured concession for them to make to a daughter who gave them as much unease as pleasure. They believed in my intelligence but doubted my judgment. My passions were too exposed, my nature too vulnerable. I might not be "broken on the wheels of life," as Miss Jenks believed. But I might well be stretched on a rack of my own making. They saw me—showing at last a public beauty—succumbing to any man who recognized it or wanted it. I doubt whether they knew the part they played in this innocence.

Whatever their fears and sadness, the plan took shape. Through friends my mother had heard of a couple who had a house near Hampstead Heath and would take in a paying guest. The husband was an art connoisseur and dealer, of Belgian origin. The wife was an English woman of breeding and charm, it was said, who was active in the cultural life of London.

Letters were copiously exchanged and the matter settled. At least, they thought with relief, she will live in a cultivated home with someone to keep a benign eye on this turbulent girl.

Expenses for bed and board were clearly set forth, and a definite limit set for extraneous spending. My boat fare and sculpture lessons, which Mrs. Reece had already arranged with an artist of "acknowledged position" in England, were of course in the budget. This was predicated for the year, or at least, nine months, on the thousand dollars left me by my late grandparents for college, matched by a second from my mother and father. It seemed to me—as it was—generous and munificent.

• • •

The going was hard. In a heavy cold rain we drove down the dreary West Side avenues to the pier, silent for once. My mother, her face drawn, I knew, from a sleepless night, was battling tears. Finally Father said, "Don't forget to check the engine room" (Leopold's first act on boarding any boat).

"If you need more sweaters," said my mother, "they have wonderful ones in London. Cheaper than here!"

We followed a porter on the long cold pier, my steamer trunk and two bags on his trolley.

"Beautiful ship," said my father. "I like Cunard funnels." I was both excited and miserable. I had never been away from my family more than a few days or so since I was born. No boarding school, no college. I wished they were not there so I couldn't look at them.

Relief came when they recognized people they knew would be on the boat; Lloyd Osbourne, the writer stepson of Robert Louis Stevenson and his wife, and Ambassador Henry Morgenthau and his wife.

The exchange of pleasantries about their "new charge" broke some of the tension.

The boarding announcement finally came, and I begged my parents not to wait for the sailing.

They did, of course. I went up the gangplank and waved from the top, then I went below to find my cabin, hoping—against knowledge—that they would go if they did not see me.

But then I thought of them waiting and couldn't bear it. I went to the main deck and hung over the rail and there they were, with the crowd just inside the pier huddled out of the rain. Mother so small and Father so tall, waving and trying to smile.

As the gangplank pulled up and a band played on the deck, an immense anguish flooded me. I knew I was going to cry and I didn't want to be seen, so I went below.

I stayed there unpacking until I saw through the porthole that we were well in the Hudson, pointed down the bay.

Then I climbed to the top deck near the funnels and stood toward the bow at the rail facing the Jersey shore, as the ship nosed down the sullen waters. The rain and my tears were one, yet suddenly, standing alone, I felt a wave of freedom so great that I drew an enormous breath. At last, it sighed.

• • •

The trip across the Atlantic followed a familiar pattern of years except for this notable—and omnipresent—euphoria of freedom. It consisted of nothing more and nothing less than not being observed by those who knew me too well. That alone was adventure. I was me—single—unique—and others who saw me could make what they wished of me. No expectations sniffed at my heels, no lapses tweaked at my conscience.

Otherwise, no change. When I wasn't seasick and suicidal, I was ebullient and hungry. I ate like a deck hand, savored my wine, played deck tennis, read in my cabin, and was educated by my elders and betters.

The stepson of R.L.S., aware of my aspirations, kindly gave me some writing hints. The one I took most to heart was this: You will find, he said, that it is often hard to get started. Because of that, your first pages may be a kind of warm-up, feeling your way. That is, he said, as it should be. But it may not be your *real* beginning. Your real beginning, the right beginning, may be on the second, or third, or even the fourth page; and you may have to jettison the ones before it. Try it next time, he said.

Or Mr. Morgenthau, our ambassador to Turkey then, would tell me a little about the British system of government and how it worked; or about Germany after her last defeat. They were all so good to me, so anxious to help; and I never knew why.

As for my contemporaries on board, I watched them dance until my familiar wallflower role got me down and I left for bed. I was all too used to what happened at the few dances I went to during the last year at home. I would sit in a chair by the wall, skinny and pale in some peasant-embroidery dress my mother thought suitable, and—like the girl in Booth Tarkington's *Alice Adams*—pretend an inordinate interest in the room's décor or the chair's arms to hide ignoble hope in my waiting gaze. I could not bear to be asking for something that nobody wanted to give.

Well, almost nobody. I would see some lady—mother or chaperon—nudging some poor young man in my direction, he would come and bow, I would rise and enter his arms, and we would dance. For some desperate reason I seemed to draw only boys without rhythm or speech who were at least two inches shorter than me. We would plow and pump our way across the room against the beat while I tried to do what was expected of me: "draw him out." When that didn't work and I began to draw *myself* out, the end drew near. No young man—at these functions at least—ever wanted to hear what a girl thought or felt about anything except him. Her response, breathlessly sprinkled with "Gosh!" or "Really?" or "How swell!" was the tribal language, proof that she belonged.

Acutely aware of this, and in spite of a passion for dance which I dared indulge only in solitary improvisations (the great Isadora?), I avoided the ballroom—and ignominy. It took another year before my idea of ultimate heaven was to dance in the arms and close to the body of a man forever, and without words.

By then, of course, the flower had left the wall.

• • •

A subsequent letter to my parents described this solo flight more explicitly (and more in terms of this particular ghost) than I could now:

Thursday

Dearests,

Tuesday afternoon was hell. The weather was so dirty that the big boat just wallowed. Rain made the decks uninhabitable, and the sea was a mass of boiling gray lava. I had a tête-à-tête lunch with the Honorable Morgenthau, the conversational interest of which kept me upright. Later in the day, however, I succumbed to the nasty gyrations, went to bed, wondered why on earth I left the comforts of home, rang for the stewardess, ate beef sandwiches and olives while prone, read awhile, then fell asleep. Wednesday found me my chipper little self once more. The sun shone, and I actually took a bath. Then, up to the deck with Halfway House and a light heart. We have a table with Homer St. Gaudens, a very nice man (artist, producer, collector, and heaven knows what else) and his wife (not so good), thus insuring plenty of amusement. In the afternoon, I played a violent set of deck tennis with St. Gaudens, the outcome of which was a tie. Thence to the swimming bath with the latter and Ethel, where we disported ourselves gaily. The pool doesn't come up to the *Reliance* one. It's on E deck, and, I think, smaller. Also, one has to pay 2/6 in order to bathe in the "mixed" hour. Henceforth I shall stick to my own sex and relinquish this expensive promiscuity.

On the whole, I prefer the *Reliance* and *Resolute,* especially as regards food and bathrooms. These are so stuffy that I have to hurry for safety's sake, and you know how I hate that. Everything is frightfully ornate and gorgeous, especially the passengers at dinner. The officers are Adonical but tantalizingly exclusive. Anyway, my predatory instincts are at low ebb on the ocean (thank God, say you!).

I'm sorry, Leopold, but I can't get the gumption to run around and investigate everything for you. All I know is that the outer rivets are about two inches in diameter, and that the toilet works by a push button. To work the electric light you push a little metal nob (diameter $\frac{1}{16}$ of an inch) up and down, down and up. See?

I had a long and informative literary talk with Lloyd this morning. He'll be a great help. He wants to take me to plays and discuss them technically with me, so that I can get on to the mechanics of the stage. He will also bring me in contact with Sir Arthur Wing Pinero *et alii.*

The damn boat's beginning to roll again and the cabin's hot as the deuce, so I'll stop for the present.

• • •

The remaining days of the voyage were so terrible that I could not possibly think of writing. The *Aquitania* is the worst cork afloat. She almost turned over. For about 24 hours I stayed in bed, bandied around so continually that I could have shrieked. Every fiber creaked and groaned and the racket became almost intolerable. Ethel was much more miserable than I, spending almost three nerve-racking days on her back. I wasn't really seasick, merely wretchedly uncomfortable and sort of bruised up. But I revived finally, got accustomed to the roll, and, champagne playing a major role in my recovery, came down to all the meals after Saturday afternoon. I have improved immensely, though. I never turned a hair while all the tables had racks on, and all liquids spilled from overturned bottles.

The Morgenthaus were lovely to me; she, by sending in to my cabin all manner of cookies and candies (then they nearly made me puke), he by talking to me and amusing me with spirited recitals of his diplomatic adventures. He introduced me to several very nice people on the boat, among whom was a pleasant and innocuous young publisher (married), a partner in Doubleday, Page, who talked books incessantly with Lloyd. I got much dope. I like the literary aroma—for a change!

Oh the Scilly Isles, portals of my new realm! Green, moss green, yellow green in the cobalt sea! Every time, every trip, leaning over the rail, sea wind in the hair, the marvelous salt damp, while we looked at the first land in nine days—the flowering earth. I could swear I smelled those flowers in the wind; I was wild with joy.

And later Southampton and the dear gray houses of England, the clutter of ships and again, that smell of Britain. What was it, even a mile from the pier, that English smell? Of smoke from coal, of hedgerows, of fields of grain and poppies, of private and brilliant gardens, of Harris tweed?

I inhaled it—the breath of freedom, of change, of adventure: life itself.

And the train from Southampton to London; those lovely trains. I was still the charge of my kindly shipboard friends, but so enraptured, as always of England's country, so near the ultimate leap, that I didn't care. I was already alone.

We got into London at about eleven o'clock. I felt very pathetic and Ethel said I looked so. You know the stuff: Poor young thing left alone in the big city ——. When we got off the train, of course I started wandering around anxiously in search of a large fair lady with short yellow hair. I was almost despairing when an official accosted me with a, "Is your name Miss Manning, or Manners?" and as I assented, a youngish gentleman approached and introduced himself as Mr. H-R., apologizing for the absence of his wife, who, he explained was too weary to come. The Osbournes handed me over to him and departed for their flat where a hot dinner awaited them. My guardian was most strangely garbed. He wore a very high, wing collar with a dark red stock, a shirt made of a porous material that reminded me strongly of BVDs, and an old felt hat cocked on the side of his head. He looks amazingly like a taller, fairer Leo Godowsky, with the addition of an English accent and tortoise-shell glasses. (At home and around Hampstead he invariably wears a monocle.) He escorted me to a huge taxi, then went after my luggage, which he procured in its entirety. Within fifteen minutes we were discussing modern art and human nature, and agreed on everything. We were fast friends when we finally chugged up a narrow street into an old square and stopped before a high brick wall, on the door of which was painted "Lawn House." Then a sense of green lawn and sweet moist smells, and a ray of warm light streaming from the threshold, on which stood a radiant creature with a mop of short, gold-wire hair. This was D., the essence of cordiality and friendliness. The young couple took me upstairs immediately, and into my spacious sitting room where a gas fire burned effectively. They made me lie down (everything reeled horribly, whether from sea legs or champagne or both I'm not quite certain) and brought a cup of steaming tea and a plate of cookies for my sustenance. I felt remarkably cheerful—as if I were in a sort of very pleasant dream. My eyes were never so dry. I knew in a moment that all was well, that I was the luckiest kid alive.

The cable sent to my father read CHAMPAGNE CAVIAR CRIMSON: our secret code for superlatives.

The letters that followed during this winter and spring tell far more honestly—without guile or restraint—what the year did to me and for me than I could now.

Swinging from rhapsody to bumptious arrogance, from total acceptance to total rejection through the familiar snap-judgments which now make me cringe, these excerpts may show at least the gradual growth from inward to outward, the beginning of Being rather than dreaming, that marked this year. It may also serve as a picture of England in the prewar placidity of power and position, and of a certain society of artists and writers then in their prime. Though my days began with the hour-long bus ride to Hampstead to work in the studio of sculptor Dobson, a succession of evening parties dazzled my attention as innocent-at-large.

Monday night, the occupants of Lawn House went to a twenty-oner at the house of Alan Gardner, the Egyptologist. The above is a party given to a young man, this time Rolph Gardner, the son, upon the event of his twenty-first birthday. A number of very callow but decent Cambridge youths were there, and many rather simple girls. Rolph himself is an amiable, bright boy, and quasi poet in that he has published a book or two of execrable verse and acts the part to perfection. Long blond hair, mincing gait, and frequent mopping of the brow; also rather pallid and pimply complexion. The entertainment consisted of dancing to a rotten piano player, eating a huge supper and drinking champagne, setting off fireworks in the garden (Guy Fawkes, you know) then more exercise. I had a fairly hard time making conversation with every youth I came across until

I settled on a definite line of Anglo-American comparison and used it unswervingly. Their chief topic seemed to be folk dancing, of all things! That recreation evidently plays a large part in English college life. And yet I've never seen a more awkward bunch of males in my life. Most of them fell all over themselves and had quavering falsetto voices in addition. However, they were perfectly nice and well mannered, which is saying a lot. We returned home about 3:30 A.M.

Monday, March 3

Friday night I went with D. to a very amusing party at the house of some friends of hers. There were about five good-looking young men there, and four charming females, besides several older people. First the hostess, her husband, and some others treated us with a performance of Barrie's *The Twelve-Pound Look*. It was sincerely done but dragged in parts. I don't much care for the play itself, but amateur theatricals always amuse me. After that, the best part came. The hostess read aloud short fairy stories, cast the people in the characters, and made them act out everything she read. If she said, "The king rode through the forest," whoever impersonated that gentleman had to pretend to gallop through the forest. The first story was "Snow White," in which the title role was assigned to me, and I had a marvelous time coughing up poisoned apples and the like. My next part was the title role of "Sleeping Beauty," from which I derived much enjoyment due to the realistic manner in which a handsome young art student woke me up. The final chef-d'oeuvre was a movie of Bluebeard's Wives—all pantomime and very exaggerated. The H.Y.A.S. was B.B. and I was one of the unfortunate wives. He was so violent in murdering me that I split up the side and had to pull myself together while dead. I hope no one noticed. They all think I'm meant for the "cinema"! Anyway, I succeeded in reducing them to hysterics, which, is all that's wanted. Pretty good idea for a party, isn't it? One could have really interesting stories to act out, like De Maupassant and his ilk.

The first morning of my nineteenth year was spent in the studio of Dobson, sculptor, in the arduous task of cutting down a block of stone to a required size with the aid of two chisels and two hefty mallets alternately used. I enjoyed myself hugely doing this purely menial work, even though my wrist is still weak from the effort. Believe me, sculpture is great exercise. I stood and hacked away for two and a half hours. I was absolutely famished when I reached Hampstead after an hour's bus ride and stowed away an incredible amount. Dobson is terribly nice. He has a sense of humor and sympathy; *and* leaves one alone. He interrupted me during the morning only once or twice to show me how to put a patina on bronze fresh from the foundry. He heated up the little bronze figure with a gas flame until it steamed, then painted it with a greenish copper solution. The resulting finish was a beautiful rich brown-gold—very satisfying and gorgeous.

• • •

I forgot to tell about my lunch at the 1917 Club! It was most interesting. All the women had stringy short hair and wore sloppy clothes and smoked incessantly, most of the men were very attractive with thick thatches of hair and strong Celtic faces. They all knew each other and all were violently excited about the election. Bob Trevelyan, the poet, was there, and also Mr. Simon, the publisher, who says that since he joined the club he's become an ardent conservative. Simon, Marik Kallin, and

I are all of the monarchist party, and consequently felt rather out of place in that den of labour and anarchy. I admire them for their sincerity but I'm positive they're on the wrong track.

I divided yesterday morning into hard intellectual and physical labor by making a start on third act, then for ¾ of an hour practicing lunging with the foil at a piece of plastecine, about 2 inches in diameter, stuck on the wall at exactly the height of an opponent's heart. I got so that I could jab it in the middle every time, with my hind foot about 8 feet from the plastecine. Besides this I shadow-fenced, jumping around defending myself against imaginary enemies, then attacking the wall at odd intervals. Miss D. used to fence, and I shall try her. She said she was good, but from her heaviness of body and the way she handled the foil, I think I could beat her. I also did all the gymnastics I could think of. Everyone here marvels at my strength! I tried games of throwing, pulling, pushing, etc., on Kitty and D. and got them both every time. And K. is ladies' skiing champion of Great Britain! You never saw me stand on my neck, did you? Or make a bridge with my stomach upward? Or touch my armpit with my big toe? Or sit like Buddha?

Three more strenuous stone-cutting hours at Dobson's Wednesday morning. The chips fly faster every time and I think the master noticed improvement. He told me to make a plastecine model at home and bring him drawings of it, so that he could determine the right sort of stone in which to execute it, so I spent the afternoon in my cheerful sitting room modeling a small female figure in a queer attitude and rather a planular, cubistic style. She is an improvement over my former boneless style, but Dobson will probably flick it away with his little finger. This morning was consumed in finishing up the lady. She looks fair in certain lights and from a few angles, but she's too damn small—due to Dobby's orders.

Tuesday

Down to Dobson through the yellow fog with my model and the sketches of it tucked under my arm. He surveyed the figure carefully from all sides and said; "That's all right. You can put it in stone. You will cast it Wednesday. Yes, you've got a design there," suggested one or two very slight changes and sent me back to my block which I rubbed with sand steadily from 2:30 to 5:30. He certainly doesn't commit himself! Anyway, he hasn't scalped me yet.

When I issued from the studio, the fog had thickened and I had to creep along the wall from lamp to flaring lamp to avoid collisions. Little alley rats slunk along likewise, suddenly lighted up, then disappeared into the murk. Haggard artists with long hair rushed through the dark with coat collar turned up and bent back.

That afternoon I went to Votichenko's in Wigmore Street. I thought he was married, but no one was there but the maid. I was too keen on adventure to leave, as a proper young maid should have done, and decided to chance it. The beginning was rather alarming, for I was ushered by the maid up a flight of dark steep carpeted steps into a dimly lit room crowded with precious ornaments and hung with tapestries and brocades. An Ikon, lit by a blue light, stood in a corner, and Votichenko bade me scrutinize it carefully. He then led me into another room, much like the first, showed me rings, letters, and seals of Louis XIV, pieces of gowns and a lock of hair and letters of Marie Antoinette, and other bits of ancient and beautiful court paraphernalia. He lives in the 18th century. I then poured tea for him, and we talked for a considerable time—about psychology, men, women, myself, himself. He was quite interesting in spots, but a little too earnest and continental for comfort—wanting me to be his friend and all that. He is Russian, black-haired, dark-eyed and handsome. We spoke in French, and I managed to be adequately cool and self-assured in that language, fortunately. Finally, he played his marvelous old instrument, the tympanon, forerunner of the piano. He used many different string-strikers and produced a wonderful variety of tonal effects. The sound of the thing was really fascinating, and I'm very glad to have heard it. I shouldn't wonder if it were the only instrument of its kind in existence. It is, I believe. Before I left, he clamped a silver and black enamel bracelet on my arm, saying it was only an impersonal gift (so I couldn't refuse it) and begged me to call up and see him again; which I won't, because, although his conduct was most gentlemanly, I don't trust him. He's rather in love with me, I'm afraid. As I went he kissed my hands twice most passionately. I was relieved to get out, but I'm very glad I did it. Experience is invaluable.

• • •

I'm furious because Clive Bell came to see John yesterday afternoon while I was at the market. Perhaps you know that nearly everybody here loathes Bell. D., who is too healthy-minded to live, can't breathe the same air with him. It seems that Henry James calls him a "parcel of filth," and he evidently fits the title. He, his wife, his former wife, Duncan Grant, Maynard Keynes, the economist, and Lopokova, the ballet dancer, change off living with one another and no one knows whose child is which or vice versa. Some menage. And withal, they accuse Bell of superficiality and popularity-mongering even in his writing. There I begged to differ. *Art* is hardly a superficial, popular book. But the H-Rs and their friends all worship Roger Fry, who, they say, is the moving artistic spirit in England and the great prophet of whom Clive Bell is merely an imitative disciple.

I'm off to Bonar Law's funeral at Westminster with John and private tickets. D. knew the family, you see. More political graft for yours truly! I put on somber garbage, then waited for John.

Lord, in Heaven, when he finally appeared, I nearly fainted. He wore an exquisite topper, morning coat, striped trousers, and carried pearl gray gloves in one hand, an amber cane in the other, and his monocle in his right eye. Beau Brummell isn't in it. We took the tube to Westminster, then walked by a colossal crowd, or rather through it, passed the police barrier, then marched grandly up the walk to the cathedral and magnificently up the aisle within. Our seats were right among those of all the M.P.s and Lords, who occupied about twenty pews solid. I was almost the only female there, and felt very timid and on my best behavior. The whole service was very impressive and really sad. Everyone thought a great deal of Law. He made a tremendous sacrifice, and is honestly loved for it. The Prince of Wales was one of the pallbearers, and stood facing us during the ceremony only about five yards away. Having an unobstructed view, I tried to catch his eye, and jolly well succeeded too—though he may not have noticed it! We saw the huge white head of Balfour, also a pallbearer, looming up ahead of us, and glimpses of Asquith, MacDonald (Leader of Opposition) and a pack of well-known baronets. These old English statesmen are a magnificent bunch of men physically—fine, massive heads, tall, erect figures, clean and generous features, and the real Saxon ruddiness. I don't wonder at English sanity when I see the men that run the empire. They may be pigheaded, but they're thoroughbreds.

The only amusing thing in the funeral was the person of Sir Douglas Hogg, some big legal pot (to be English), who marched up with the officiating prelates attired in a ridiculous little wig, several sizes too small, that looked as if it had been made of waste. His name is well justified by his winy nose, beery jowls, and bulging eyes. We made a grand recessional (when the service was over) down the nave, accompanied by the clanging of the chimes and Chopin's inevitable. Our exit was as public as our entrance. Some of our neighboring M.P.s and Peers parted from us and went back to the House. Others went home. I loved to see their shining toppers and beautiful spats disappear into the mist.

• • •

In the evening Bernard Adeney came in to cheer up, having just seen his wife successfully through a very serious operation. He was all in and looked haggard, but after a liqueur and a glass of port, together with absorbing conversation on personality in art, and the horror of war, brightened perceptibly. It is terrible what these fine men went through in the war. Most of them, being essentially creative, were dead against it and had to suffer the tortures of the damned in the struggle between ostracism and the business of murdering humans. A young man like John, only twenty-six, ages ten years in the war, and comes back a middle-aged, shattered being. He fits in neither with the young men nor the old. All his contemporaries are killed. Then, by God, he has to listen to the murmurs and rumblings presaging more war, more destruction.

The hoarfrost has thickened this morning, and the limit of visibility contacted to ten feet. My windows frame blankness. The blankness is turning yellow. What next, O lord?

(Another Party)

Clive Bell, moon-faced, eye-browless, blond-haired; Duncan Grant, a fascinating youngish man with rumpled black hair, dark blue eyes and a very sensitive, mobile mouth; Maynard Keynes, the great economist, a dark and stronger Dudley Hale in appearance; Vanessa Bell, Clive's wife and Duncan Grant's painting partner, an attractive, simple woman to look at; Walter Sickert, the great wit of the artists; Osbert Sitwell, the poet (so-called); Francis Birrell, one of the brilliant young writers in England; Virginia Woolf, well-known author of powerful impressionist novels; David Garnett (who I unfortunately did not see), the author of *Lady into Fox.* The fifty or sixty other people consisted of aspiring young artists in bright blue shirts, excessively homely women, freaks of nature, and observers like D. and me. Fry, Sickert, Bell, Keynes, Sitwell, Birrell, and Woolf gave incredibly brilliant and witty speeches. I have never heard such scintillation before; nor such petty vindictiveness and personal allusions. The woman, again, was the only speaker free from small private animosities. Dobson, drunk as a fish, gave a rather funny but totally pointless speech, and poor Adeney, who had never spoken in public and was scared stiff, stumbled through a few colorless words of thanks. He tried desperately to get drunk but couldn't pull it off. He's too much of a gentleman and too little of an artist. Due to an impossible male bore on my left and a wall on my right, and a strong sense of being "out of it" entirely, I didn't enjoy myself as much as I did at the literary dinners. These artists are frightfully cliquey and greater snobs than any baronet, especially the Bloomsbury set (Bell, Grant, Keynes etc.). Clive was surprisingly cheap and slanderous in his speech, however witty. Evidently his purism and asceticism are confined to the province of art only.

Arranged to meet J. and D. for a big dinner being given in honor of Rakovsky, the Soviet ambassador spurned by Curzon and taken in by the Labour Party, and Frank Wise, the English head of the Co-operative Scheme in Russia, an economic genius and a great humanitarian. Nevinson, the great journalist, and Brailsford, another prominent writer and wit, were there. The club was jammed with homely but interesting men and women all violently excited about the election, in which the Labour gains are positively astounding. The Conservatives are literally being pushed out of the field by the Liberals and Labourites and even the Liberals are losing ground.

After coarse but ample fare, we all adjourned to a large barnlike room on the top of the house and settled down to hear Rakovsky and Wise speak. The Russian spoke in guttural and broken, though very clear, French, and stressed the necessity of co-operation between Russia and England. Both countries wanted peace and both should and must combine to maintain it by economic intercourse. Wise extolled the Soviet regime and emphasized Rakovsky's theme. Both spoke well, the latter charmingly, but neither told us anything new or suggested anything specifically constructive. Many of their remarks were greeted with wild clapping, low "hear, hear," and scornful grunts and laughs. These last expressions always followed any mention of Churchill, Curzon, or the English newspapers. The sight of that bare room filled with smoke and people and lighted by a merciless unshaded bulb, with Rakovsky's Napoleonic head and Wise's black-haired Celtic face rising above the attentive mass, will never leave my mind.

• • •

The hideous Queen's Hall was packed to overflowing and wild with excitement at the prospect of seeing Weingartner and hearing Casals. Should it interest you, the program was as follows: *Egmont Overture,* Mozart *Symphony in E flat,* Dvořák *Violoncello Concerto,* and the Brahms *C minor Symphony.* Weingartner was really extraordinary. I have never seen such stick technique. He was very restrained but tremendously dynamic and effective. He was sort of master of every instrument there. And such hands! The orchestra was a little rough (that's the term, I believe?) but undoubtedly at its best under him. Then little Pablo trotted in. He played the first two bars in a horrible, rasping tone, then suddenly stopped short. Weingartner, his stick poised in mid air, stopped. The orchestra faded out. Pablo seemed to be fiddling with his bow, and made agonized faces at Weingartner. The two whispered awhile, then Casals stood up and said in a weak but distinct voice, "I am very sorry, but I have a cramp in my left arm and cannot continue now," and made his exit amid applause. After an intermission, the Brahms was played, then Pablo returned and went through the Dvořák successfully. I thought I'd go back and tell Pablo that if he worked hard he might be able to play the cello very well someday; that he had unmistakable signs of talent!

[Note: I did go back, but I did not call him Pablo. My awe of him was, as it is, boundless. M.M.]

After lunch I went down to the National Gallery and took in too much, as usual. I tried to concentrate on De Predis, Botticelli, Boltraffio. Tintoretto, and Della Francesca, but soon found myself comparing the brush techniques of Rembrandt, Hals, Rubens, and Van Dyck, and rushing up hectically to their pictures to get closer views. I could write a monograph on the results of my observations but haven't the patience. I had a solitary tea at home and then embarked on the first act of my latest spasm. This is the life. I don't think I shall ever be able to live a dependent existence again. This freedom has made me very good-natured and my hair curl. I'm afraid you will find me insufferable when I return to the fold! But don't worry, I love you just as much as ever and perspective has certainly not damaged you.

• • •

What do you think of Marya (accent on first syll:) the Polish-Russian equivalent of Marie as a possible first name for me? I simply can't stick Marie. It's not *me,* and I hate signing plays and letters with such a misfit. Please think of it seriously. It really isn't a change at all, and perfectly consistent with my ancestry and type.

Oodles of love,

[My parents generously acceded to this, saying that there had indeed been discussion at my birth as to the two possible versions. "Marie" was chosen in honor of my great-aunt but had always made me feel like a French maid in a bad farce. My classmates called me Murree, my intimates Ma Mie, a contraction of "my friend (and or mistress)" in French. M.M.]

In January my hostess D. had received my parents' permission to take me for two weeks to Adelboden in Switzerland for skiing and a change from London routines and weather. We were to go with Kitty, my housemate (to be recognized forty years later as Mrs. Malcolm Muggeridge!) and to foregather there with several friends of D.'s, young and older, in a modest inn.

These weeks were boundlessly happy. Not only because of the beauty of the place and the fierce purity of mountain air, which I so loved at Pontresina years before; not only because I learned to ski, and ski well; but because I met a man whom I was to love in a strange way over a long period.

He was a Scotsman, six foot two with one of the most beautiful bodies I had ever seen and the face of his tribe: long, lean, boldly boned, with a sandy mustache and a thatch of straight sandy hair that flopped, in any exertion, over a high forehead.

He had fenced on the British Olympic team, was a rally racer, an amateur violinist, a passionate advocate of ballet, painting, and opera, and withal a man of infinite gentleness: self deprecating and shy.

His wife was an Irish sprite, small, thin, sharp-tongued and sharply pretty, a singer already embarked on a career in opera. They were a disparate though delightful couple, C. and B., often going their separate ways. With him, D. and I spent most of our days and evenings, skiing or talking or dancing at night in one of the small hotels and *Gast stuben.*

But more and more C. would take me along trails and up and down hills, teaching me as we went, showing me as he swooped and turned and I followed in fear, delight, and adoration. It was worth falling down for him to pick me up.

Neither of us said anything personal to the other, but two public occasions made words unnecessary. One was a fancy dress ball where I went as the faun in *L'après-midi.* I had painted large irregular spots on my tan ski-underwear tights, wore a close-fitting top of the same color draped with a ratty fur piece, made two golden horns that I fixed to my head with rubber bands, and painted an exaggerated ballet make-up with enormous black upturned rims to my eyes.

D. looked at me before we went out and said, "Aren't you a little overexposed? You're all leg."

The costume did indeed cause a stir, but mainly in me. C. looked at me and then we danced and the unity was absolute and dizzying. We said nothing to each other, then or later except for general chatter.

The written chatter to my parents had mentioned C. and his wife and described the former as handsome, discreet, and flawlessly attired, but my adulation of British males was by then too familiar to cause specific alarm.

Nor did this account of another party at Adelboden sound any alerts, especially as I took pains in hamming it up.

> There were lots of paper hats and favors and ridiculous stunts such as lining the women up behind a sheet and letting the men grab hold of their up-stretched hands, and making the ladies take off one shoe, throw it in a basket, and have it fitted on by whatever male happened to find it. In this latter affair a strange thing happened. The basket with about fifty evening slippers was placed in the middle of the ballroom with a sheet over it. Then all the men made a mad and simultaneous rush toward it and fell on each other in a frantic effort to seize a shoe. To my astonishment, C. the perfect, reserved gentleman, bounded across the floor, dove in the midst of the struggling males, managed to extract *my* shoe, wandered around the room absent-mindedly as if to find its partner, then finally brought it sheepishly to me, mumbling something about his not knowing it was mine. Now, I have

worn those slippers every night, C. is excessively observant, and they are unique in Adelboden. The mystery is: was he bluffing or was he not?

The misery of having to leave Adelboden and C. was obviated by an invitation to join him and his wife for a few days in Milan, where they resided temporarily while she pursued her singing lessons with a favored maestro. D., highly affirmative, cabled my parents of the plan, and off we went. C. was at the station waiting for us, and led us to their hotel and subsequently into a round of new experiences marred only by our inability to be alone except for fleeting moments.

From Wednesday until Monday we were going it steadily from 10 A.M. till 12 midnight. We exhausted all the picture galleries in Milan, arguing violently on art in the abstract during the process, covered the *duomo* from top to bottom and decided it was decadent but effective, drank *cappuccinos* or chocolate about five times a day in the various attractive cafés scattered all over the city, saw the beautiful medieval *castello,* a huge Florentine-style red plaster pile with enormous and gorgeous halls filled with paintings and museum objects, heard Strauss's *Salome,* Puccini's *Gianni Schicchi* and *Traviata* and enjoyed one another's company immensely. Toscanini didn't conduct *Salome* and *Schicchi,* but they were excellently done. Salome seems so involved musically and so neurotically polyphonic that I came away with no definite conception of it as to thematic material, etc., but with a most interesting sound-chaos in my head and a desire to hear it again. The staging was superb, the singing neat but not gaudy.

This brief idyll came to an abrupt end when D. and I got back to England and Lawn House.

Cataclysmic things have happened [I wrote home]. Prepare yourself for a shock: D. came back from Switzerland to find that J. had decided to leave her and run away with Mrs. L. to Paris. I cannot describe the horror of the last few days . . . To make matters worse, Mrs. L.'s daughter is also in love in J. and will go with them. It is all a nightmare . . . with much grim comedy mixed up with it.

I shall certainly stick to D. at any price . . . Believe me, I sure am being thrown into life with a will!

What's more, Dobson has calmly left for India for three months without letting me know. This unforeseen circumstance has forced my hand and ended at last the infernal struggle between my two interests. I have decided to devote myself entirely to writing . . . and am infinitely relieved. My sculpture has been too much of the head and too little of the heart . . . an intellectual indulgence rather than a passion. Whereas the expression of any strong feeling in me is invariably in writing. Isn't that proof enough that words are my ultimate métier? I know you will be frightfully disappointed, and I'm awfully sorry about it. But my mind is absolutely clear. I think I have found myself, which after all is what I came away to do. Please don't think that I found sculping too hard and hadn't the courage or strength to go on. The work involved didn't frighten me in the least. But I refuse to be perfunctory in anything. Tepidity and indifference are an insult to any art and in the end killing to their owner. You will probably say, "Think again before you take this big step; you are probably in a state of temporary discouragement." And you will be wrong. I have thought again—and again and again and again. And I am not discouraged.

This letter provoked considerable alarm at home. There were family conclaves, I heard, in which my conservative aunts counseled my immediate removal from an unstable atmosphere and sources of contamination, etc. etc., but where my parents prevailed in the belief that I was strong enough to weather reality, however unpleasant. D. wrote them begging that I be allowed to stay, that no radical change in living would occur, and that she needed me.

And indeed, life did continue very much as before. I began to realize, perhaps for the first time, that the "ideal" marriage was not ideal at all, and that tensions had been deliberately played down to maintain an equable surface. I watched D. gradually flower in freedom and confidence, and found a new strange peace in Lawn House.

For the last few days I have been working steadily on the new play, and am halfway through the second act. It promises well. "Undercurrents" and "The Microscope" are two possible titles. Besides this intensive and exciting labor, I have been typing for Marik one of his lectures—the political history in Russia since 1812—and my days have been well filled. Adeney came in after supper the other night and was as charming and sympathetic as ever. Thursday afternoon D. and I went down to see about Birley's Fencing Club, only to find that it was no more—financial failure or something—and that C.'s fencing kit had been moved over to Bertrand's, another place, about which I shall inquire. My beloved C. is very anxious for me to join the place where he works!

Roughly constructed plot of third act after much sitting and cogitation. This play is very hard work. I can't seem to make the acts long enough. The first play was also too short. I fear I must acquire the art of padding. Fenced violently in the afternoon, and in the evening went with D. to a dinner given by the London Group of artists in honor of their resigning president, Adeney. It was most amusing. To my utter horror, the first person I saw was Dobson, back from India, and very cheery. He shook my hand, asked how I was getting on, and moved away, thank God. He seemed rather sheepish. I received another blow when Dobson was announced as the next president of the Group. I'm sorry for the Group.

In the afternoon I gave rather painful birth to a rotten sonnet and another poem, fairly clever but not worth much in the sum total of human affairs.

• • •

When I read of a person like Edna St. Vincent Millay, I get frightfully discouraged—scarcely nineteen when she wrote a marvelous long poem called *Renascence,* which I could never even touch, and now, only about thirty, working with the Provincetown Players etc., etc., and here I am already nineteen with a few puny little sentimental stanzas to my name. I wish some competent critic would either say, "Drop it!" or, "This is what I call poetry. Stick to it, do this and that, and there'll be some hope for you!" Hell, I don't know.

• • •

By the way, I wish you wouldn't tell me not to worry about my work or anything and to drop it if I want. It makes it very hard for both of us, since I must make my living eventually and want to. Treat me as you would a boy. I bet you never told Leopold not to worry about his music. You see, the less that's expected of you, the less you do. Expect me to write "the American play" or evolve a new sculptural technique, and I may do so. And I've seen enough homes to realize that marriage need not stop important work on the female side. Even that is so far off that why consider it! I think I have the guts, and with your backing I may do something. At present nothing worries me but my ignorance. I live, work, and enjoy myself and take what comes. Here endeth lesson number one.

• • •

Yesterday morning I worked on the play, in the afternoon I walked with D., and in the evening Molly Hamilton, a well-known political novelist and a very influential socialist and member of the Labour Party (she got 5000 votes from her constituency in the last election, but failed) came to dinner. She is a fascinating little woman, chuck-full of brains and energy and courage, a close friend of MacDonald, Leach, Snowden and all the big Labour men. She had a swine of a husband who treated her like dirt, stood him for eight years, then divorced him. Without doubt the women are the finer people here.

• • •

I'm so thrilled I can't see straight. Your little daughter actually made a hit at the Pen Club last night! But I'll start from the beginning. The dinner was at Gatti's, in the Strand. When we first came, everyone stood around talking to everyone else and greeting the newcomers. I was introduced to several big literary pots, then C. B. Fernald, the adapter of *the Mask and the Face*. *Then*—Galsworthy came in. Ethel brought me, much against my will, to him and gave him a brief biography. He shook my hand, pretended to be interested, and wished me luck—all correct and awful, poor man. He has a marvelously sensitive, pure, and distinguished face—the highest intellectual type, and it was a pleasure just to watch him.

• • •

You know, it will be hellish breaking away from people and experiences like that. You can't conceive how at home and firmly rooted I feel in London. However, ça passe. Your suggestion about my housekeeping next winter plunged me into the depths for forty-eight hours. I realize that it would be only decent of me to do it, but Oh God! I warn you, I firmly intend to get a job of some sort in N.Y.; in a publishing house, or on a magazine, or translating. You must see that outside work is essential, and I don't want to take little courses here and there and everywhere. I'm convinced of the futility of book-learning, and the immense value of actual experience. Incidentally, is it humanly possible for anyone to housekeep with Tante's superior knowledge and experience, hovering anxiously in the air? Besides, I cannot economize. You've brought me up on far too high a scale of living. If I were a boy embarking on a literary career you wouldn't dare suggest that or any equivalent job, would you? As for trying to repay you for what you've done for me, that is impossible. The only thing I can do is to try to achieve a high standard in my chosen line and be some sort of contribution to society as a personality. Unwilling housekeeping is no step toward either goal. I know I shouldn't have written all this, but I can't keep things to myself. And consequently show my worst side quite openly and calmly. Don't worry, I realize fully what a mean, disgusting creature I am, but there it is.

Housekeeping or no housekeeping, I'm dying to see you.

That mention of C. has faded from these letters is a contrary indication. He was more and more in my life, coming repeatedly to Lawn House to fence with me or take me to odd corners of the city and later, in the early marvelous flowering of English spring, to drive me in his car to country pubs and places of special beauty.

On the first of these excursions we drove after lunch by a lake through a small dirt road in woods to a grove surrounding a mossy clearing: silent, shielded, enclosed. There he made love to me; the first. With utmost gentleness, with uncanny knowledge of my nature and needs. Loving him as I did, I was drowned in joy.

Too much so then to wonder why (in the phrase of the time) he did not "go all the way." I assumed it was because of my virginity: he was being protector as well as lover. But later when I begged for total communion, he smiled and said his entire pleasure was in giving me pleasure; that was all he wanted.

Later on he said that ever since he had seen his wife give birth in agony, he could not bear the risk of impregnating any woman, of bearing responsibility for their pain and deformation. I knew he worshiped strong and tensile bodies from his talk of the ballerinas who were his intermittent mistresses. Pregnancy would, of course, destroy their careers: he could love them and leave them free.

All this he told me and I ceased to question or plead. Instinctively I felt that somewhere along the line—a wound, his wife?—something had castrated him. And because he bore this worst of all losses for a man with such dignity, such a deep capacity for love, I cherished him all the more.

We were lovers intermittently over many years, meeting in different countries (he would come to where I happened to be, no matter) free from doubt or guilt or question. Neither of us demanded more. He was bound to his wife in a complex of ties and affections, and my own life could never have accommodated to his without hurt for both.

We knew we had a very special thing and that it went very deep and needed no words.

My parents knew nothing of this. When they came for me later that spring they met C. at Lawn House and loved him too. My father talked violins with him, C. took him to his tailor, and both parents invited him to join us for a week on the Italian Riviera. He accepted: a doubtful boon since we could be alone only under Mediterranean water.

If they had known about us, however, I think they would have been grateful that their wayward daughter had such a knight—*parfit* and gentle—as lover.

Now, years after his death, I am grateful too.

• • •

In that June of 1924 when mother, father, and brother came to reclaim me, they found a huge Valkyrie with a strong British accent and a marked reluctance to leave. I found people with an awful American accent whom I adored.

It was I, of course, who had changed, and they knew it well. But the gap was quickly bridged by D. and mutual affection, and although parting from Lawn House was a major wrench, I was ready for new places and new experience. Far from closing in, life opened even wider.

My parents had rented a small villa near the then very unpretentious Hotel du Cap at Antibes for a month. We were charmed with the view of the sea, the rocks, the terraces, the flowers, the smell of the air. I lost no time swimming, diving, sunning, eating, and looking.

One later golden afternoon, my father and I were sitting at a table on the hotel terrace drinking an apéritif while we waited for Mother to change for dinner.

At a table nearby, a young man detached himself from a group and walked over to us. He was blond and delicately handsome and he bowed to father.

"Pardon me for intruding, sir," he said, "but we had been admiring you and your daughter and I won the toss as to who should find out your name."

Father smiled and told him.

"I'm Scott Fitzgerald, sir. May I sit down?"

My God, I thought, it isn't possible. He *looked* like the jacket cover on *Beautiful and Damned,* but these things didn't happen.

A waiter passed by and Fitzgerald ordered another round before Father could stop him.

"I also, Mr. Mannes, wanted to ask you a special favor. We'd like to borrow your daughter and take her to Juan-les-Pins tonight, after dinner—to the Casino."

Father looked at me. I don't think he knew who this was. I looked at him with fervent spaniel eyes, panting.

"I promise, sir, that we will get her back safely and not too late."

"I will hold you to that, Mr.—." *"Fitzgerald,"* I hissed. "Mr. Fitzgerald . . . on your word as a gentleman!"

The writer rose, giving a parting bow. "Thank you, sir." And to me, "May we pick you up about nine in the hotel lobby?"

I nodded, speechless, and then enlightened my parent. Fortunately he had not followed Scott's more flagrant exploits in print, and I prayed that my mother would not enlarge on them. We had all seen the blond and beautiful triad—Zelda and Scott and the baby girl—playing on the beach and splashing in the water; and Father said he had talked to Zelda before he knew who she was, and found her charming.

• • •

About eight of us, in two cars, drove through the aromatic night to the Casino at Juan-les-Pins: a place full of gaiety, not at all like the night clubs in New York, I thought.

We talked, we drank, we danced, we laughed. I was so dazzled by being in his company that I remember nothing he said; and nothing specific anyone did, until suddenly, dancing, I saw Zelda climb on our table and start to dance. It was part hula, part her own invention, and people began to stop what they were doing to stare. Not merely because she was dancing on the table (they knew her spirit) but because she was lifting her skirts higher and higher above her knee, with no evidence of anything beneath.

People began to laugh and clap and Zelda laughed, swinging her golden hair around her face. Scott was not laughing: he begged his wife to stop, to come down; but it seemed to me that she didn't even see him; her face was blind.

When the skirts were flipping above her crotch, Scott—with the help, I am sure, of Gerald Murphy, pulled her—struggling fiercely—down from the table. Someone got our wraps from the vestiaire while the two men propped and dragged the resistant, drunken, Zelda—shouting and slurring—through the Casino doors.

At the top of the stone steps just outside the door was an oriental rug about six by eight feet large. Zelda broke away from her captors and crawled beneath it, humped and twitching like some playful beast.

Now no one laughed. I was frightened: I had never seen anything like this before. And she was beautiful.

Scott went on his knees and pled with her to come out, again and again, but only silence or muffled giggles answered him.

She was finally pulled out and half carried to their car while Scott made a point of seeing that I went with others.

My parents were still awake when I got home, but beyond saying that I had a lovely time, I told them nothing. I couldn't bear to betray my new friends. The next afternoon the pair were their golden selves, and in the following days I would see Father listening earnestly to Zelda. Women loved him for this: not only his looks and grace, but how he listened kindly, and never judged.

A few nights later, well after midnight, the telephone shattered our sleep in the villa. Father answered and the call was brief: Scott asking Father to come to their room, Zelda was in a bad way and Scott couldn't handle it.

My father changed from pajamas into trousers and shirt, accompanied by the murmurings of my mother. These changed to alarmed protest when I too dressed: I should not be exposed to such things, it was no place for me.

But I went with Father to the Fitzgerald rooms in the hotel. I stood by the door while Scott led Father into their bedroom where Zelda thrashed and screamed on their double bed. The only words I could make out were "I want chaos! Give me chaos! I want chaos!"

Father sat down on a chair by the bed and took one of her hands in one of his while he stroked her twitching head with the other. "No, you don't, Zelda," he said, again and again. "That's not what you want," and he said other things I didn't hear.

Scott stood by, white as paper, looking at Zelda. Once he said to Father, "I'm sorry I had to wake you, Mr. Mannes, but you were the only person who might . . ."

Finally Zelda was relatively still; moving and murmuring a little, her forehead wet with sweat, her eyelids slowly fluttering into rest.

My father stood up. "I think she'll be quiet now," he said to Scott. "I hope she will."

On the way back from the hotel my father said, "It's tragic, isn't it? They have so much to give, and she is so lost . . ."

• • •

It was, in every way, an incredible month. A beautiful young Italian panted after me, an old Italian breathed heavily in my ear, E. Phillips Oppenheim spoke to me when he wasn't floating in his pool big belly upward in his favorite position, and Rockwell Kent asked me to run away with him to Paris. I believed everything everybody said and wondered what on earth I could say or do.

Evasive banter and sudden flights balked the Italians, but Kent was then not only a famous painter but a persuasive man, and his intensity scared and fascinated me. I would get little notes in his tiny beautiful hand, saying wonderful things.

And then there was Shuggy, Sir Hugo de Bathe, husband of Lillie Langtry, the "Jersey Lily" decades before. He lived in a villa with a regimental friend called Pinky and several monkeys, and looked the "Perfect Model of a Modern Major General," Retired.

Shuggy would follow me down to the daily swim, pausing to chat. And then one day, out of the blue, he suggested marriage.

He said he would have me painted by Lavery, I would ride in a carriage with five balls (I couldn't understand that until I saw his crest), and that he didn't care if I had other and younger men so long as I lived with him to comfort his later years.

I was stunned. I started to stutter something about a boy back home (had indeed met the youth I would later marry) but he said, rising, "Ye know, my dear, there's still a lot of life left in me, let's dive from the rock, eh-what?"

The rock was thirty feet above the water and scary even to me, although I dived from it. But insist he did, to my dismay.

It was warranted. Sir Hugo gave a little jump, pointed downward, hit the water, and disappeared from sight.

The Italian Adonis, who was standing by, and I dived in; found him bubbling slowly to the surface, flanked him like porpoises, and brought him up. We pulled him out of the water and onto the raft, which took some doing. Frightened, we watched him gasping his way back into breath, eyes closed, limbs wholly inert. I heard him later make some whispered quip: "Poor show, eh what?"

There was nothing funny about it; any of it. In fact, I felt full of pity and shame, being the cause.

• • •

Reality closed in again in the fall of that year. The ride up Tenth Avenue from the steamship pier was a familiar shock, absorbed only gradually within the refuge of home.

The year in old civilizations made the new one even uglier than I had remembered; Tenth Avenue was its squalid and brutal portal. Why did we have these tenements with their zigzag fire escapes, why the eyeless warehouses, why those cluttered signs on cluttered treeless streets?

Once home, especially now on the East Side, the squalor receded from the minds of those not forced to live in it. The refuge, now paper thin, was then substantial. We could shut out what we did not see, while total vision is now forced upon us—one way or another.

So life ostensibly resumed a familiar pattern. No school, of course, but I lived again with my parents for two main reasons. One was that they could not afford a separate apartment for me. The other was that in spite of my rebellious independence—by now if anything deepened—I realized that life at home was not only more interesting but far more comfortable than anything I could create for myself.

"Life at home" was not confined to the four of us and our friends, however absorbing. The social focus of my youth was the brownstone on East Sixty-first Street where my ebullient uncle, Walter Damrosch, and his wife, the former Margaret Blaine, kept open house with their four daughters for the most talented and witty people of that time. There was no age division. Fifteen to seventy, it made no difference if you had something to give; and diversions like charades or word games or skits brought us—often hilariously—together.

My uncle was always center-stage: charming host and perfect showman, setting the party mood with rousing pianistic flourishes or calls to action. I loved him even when I could not help knowing the diminutions my father suffered from the brighter musical spotlight cast on his brother-in-law, or comparing the dominant values of success that prevailed in this convivial home with the serious questioning of them in our own as standards of worth.

Essentially a loner, moreover, I resisted the "clan" concept, averse to being sucked into even this glamorous company. In groups I felt vulnerable and even alien.

For at nineteen I was still retarded in three ways: domestically, sexually, and politically. I could not cook, I had not been breached, I was totally ignorant of the forces that ordered or moved the society and the nation.

The faces of Presidents, Coolidge and then Hoover, did not interest or appeal, the speeches of politicians in the papers I never read, and the Market had only one meaning: food.

Life consisted of men and writing.

At this point I decided to put down in black and white just what I had accomplished in the second category during the last year, in England and New York. The comments, of course, are my own.

Opera Literata
a
Maria Mannesus

1924

They That Have Eyes	Drama in three acts. Idea excellent, execution pitiful.
Island of Desire	Comedy in three acts. Unfinished. Open sewer.
Cloistered (?)	Educational comedy in one act. Amusing idea, heavily done.
The Russians	Long poem in six parts. Several superb passages.
Quartet	Drama in three acts. Fairly trite and decidedly boring, though better in form.
Going the Rounds	Melodrama in one act. Rather pat, but not too original or epoch-making.

Sea Change	Comedy in three acts. Brilliant idea very crudely and poorly presented. Amusing scenes. Burned up.
Variations on a Theme	Long poem in three parts . . . Good.
In the Blood (?)	Comedy in three acts, third act unfinished. Amusing idea, but too thin and superficial for a long play.

1925

Foul Is Fair	Ironic comedy in three acts. Quite brilliant and original. Technique better but still uncertain and ragged.
Everyman	
Sense (?)	Long poem. Luscious in sound, but as usual too youthfully rich.
Emancipation	Essay. Straight stuff.
Mountains	Comedy in one act. Original idea fairly well presented.
Book reviews, translation, philosophy.	
Help	Three-act comedy of kitchen life. Ghastly result of Milton trying to write bedtime stories. Let's not speak about it.
Book reviews for New Republic	
Charge 999	Article for Junior League. Sharp and well-written diatribe against "doing good."

Degas, Sculptor Rue la Boétie	Two lone articles on art. Well written, but too dogmatic.
Birth of a Neurotic Fifth Avenue at Noon Impressions of a Lady at a Burlesque Monologue	Short psychological experiments, indifferently good. Several new ideas and many old ones.
The Young God	Short story. Quite poetic and masterful. No excess luggage. Complete.
First Officer Stuart	Short story. Neat plot, but more for Ladies' Home Companion. Not poetry.
There Is a Love	Very short story. Best of all in elimination. Also, original and subtle.
Compensation	Long philosophic poem. Aristocratic idea and treatment.
The Shadow	One-act play for children. Interesting attempt to write something in which a child could find adventure and a grown-up irony. Double-faced. Fairly successful, I think.
The Manneses in Heaven	Short skit on family failings, written for Christmas. Funny to "those who know."

It must be clear by now that with the exceptions of one play and some reviews, these efforts died on the vine. The tendrils of hope curling upward in England—the encouraging, kind words from professional people—drooped into failure.

Most of the plays I tried out on my family. They must have been pretty terrible: even those meant to be serious convulsed them. They wept from laughing.

I comforted myself that they were too daring, too advanced for my parents and the time; and at the least, they entertained. I suspect that these amateur forays and fragments might have been hailed three decades later as Happenings, ideal for the mindless tatters that pass for theater.

No matter, I went on—why I will never know. Why did I keep on *doing* them? Who *read* them? They were piled away and forgotten.

And so was the journal I had been keeping month after month.

I hope this daily drewling will help my style. That's the chief reason for my doing it. I want to attain such ease of expression that the medium will take care of itself, allowing the idea to be paramount. As it is, my ideas are much too good for my execution. Philosophically I am trusting to time to ameliorate this condition.

Incredible, foolish as it may seem, I think the unconscious mission in the lives of most people is to discover the ultimate Good in others; to justify human existence. One year ago I would have protested scathingly that our attitude toward and interest in other people was that purely of curiosity; or that of action and reaction. But I am convinced it is not so. I am intensely conscious now of searching for a certain spark of divinity, a certain flame, in every person I meet. And if it is not there, or seems not to be, I come away sorely disappointed. That is the standard, and the only standard, with which I measure my fellow beings.

• • •

Heartbeats is time; the inward pulsation that causes outward beauty is Rhythm.

• • •

The day of little painted squares hung on walls is passing. It is up to the artists to adapt their creation to modern life; to make it more vital, more essential, more bound up with human living. We are passing more and more from the particular to the general; from a family to a nation, from a nation to a league of nations, from a house to a city. Gone are the days of close-knit, inwrought, homes, towns, and countries. And since life is no longer bounded by hedgerows and great stone walls, painting should not be bounded by wooden frames. I am not yet big enough to find the solution. But perhaps no one is. Such solutions find themselves. And that process of discovery is evolution.

March 22nd

During the last year or two I have often been on the verge of discovering some ultimate truth. When some creation of man or evidence of man's divinity lifts me into ecstasy, I feel a sudden acute clarification of some sixth, perceptive sense, and seem on the threshold of revelation. It is intoxicating, tantalizing, wonderful. I lose consciousness, and allow the subconscious to rise higher and higher until it nearly reaches the conscious level; while I, knowing it could bring great wisdom, try desperately to give it free rein. And then, just as I am *beginning* to see and to understand, the sixth sense slips away, and the mystery is unsolved. It happened last night in the Greek room at the Museum while César Franck streamed in with tragic exaltation. I was alone, gazing at the lordly Greek and Roman heads in a sort of daze, passionately adoring their broad brows and splendid heads, and sensitive mouths. When suddenly they all came alive and listened silently, intently to the music. And I seemed to see in a flash the whole human evolution—the whole pathetic struggle—the divine comedy—and my heart was filled with a huge compassion. But the meaning of the vision escaped.

So I continued dreaming, endlessly typing, and planning for greatness. I could not endure the thought of obscurity. And because this seemed to me the condition of most women, I would not be like them; surrounded for life by dirty dishes, dirty clothes, and whimpering children. Tied to only one man, beholden to him and less than him. I had seen it, hadn't I, in the homes of friends? They claimed they were happy, they said (with pride) this was what a woman was for. They assured me that I would finally realize this happiness too.

I rejected them fiercely, sustained by a new confidence and a new passion. During the year I had fallen in love with the race of men and felt free to show it.

Wherever I went I looked at the contour of their mouths, the set of their ears against their heads, the way their hair grew on their napes, the texture of their skins, the shape of their hands, the way they walked, the set of their shoulders, and—of course—their eyes.

When I saw a man who pleased me especially I would look straight into his eyes. This would have a devastating effect in the sense that I seemed ready for him when in fact I was not. The way I talked, the way I danced, that look in my eye spelled a sophistication, they would tell me, later belied. They could not believe that within this dancing body pressed so close, the waiting mouth, the provocative talk lay—still—such ignorance; such innocence. Some men were bent on relieving me of both, some refused to believe it and I, of course, was ashamed to confess it.

It must be remembered, however, that in that time well-bred young men did not automatically seduce supposedly well-bred girls on the first encounter or even the fourth or fifth. Girls I knew insisted, in fact, that the harder you were to get, the more "they" wanted you. It was fatal, they said, to show how you felt too soon: "they" wouldn't respect you.

I thought this dishonest and disgusting. Instead I continued to look at beautiful men adoringly and to pray that another C., or Mr. Burton (Attorney-at-Law, Boston) would initiate me into the final mysteries.

In spite of my new assurance—or possibly because of it—most young men of my own age were still frightened of me: too big, too bright, too different, too hard to handle. Why bother, when the world was full of easy, compliant, soft, and "helpless" women?

Oh, I would moan to myself, if only I were small and fluffy, or had huge breasts and no brains! How happy I would be!

(Later I yearned to be a burlesque stripper, but it seemed impractical.)

April 11, 1925

Long absence from confessional due to absorption in "Mountains" in which I have at last gotten rid of the Swiss hut idea. Everything comes out of my system sooner or later. Fortunately I have been purged of my worst rancors—namely those of Veltin and sex repression. Although, as a matter of fact, the first was not adequately treated, and the last is continually recrudescent. (I mean as subjects, not actualities!) I have a ghastly idea that I shall after all commit a novel. It's the only form suitable for an orgy of egotism and luscious language, and the world should by no means be deprived of that. Anyway, I talked to a young publisher the other night who made me promise to give him first reading, and of course the spur tickled. My only worry is that I may not have the patience to cover five hundred big sheets of paper with pencilled scrawls. And yet, others more ineffectual than I have managed it. Oh it would be rich!

Last night as I was preparing to step under the shower, these words kept singing through my head unaccountably: "I am the resurrection and the life," spoken quietly by a voice certainly not my own, yet within me; impersonal, yet having to do with me. I can't make it out. Such things are strange.

• • •

I think the drama of the future will depend on a synchronoization of sound, color, and sense.

The typewriter has a sense of humor. To wit, spelling of the longest word in the passage above, purely accidental.

During that spring I had met a Russian painter at a party, Savely Sorin. A portraitist of international repute (they said), he asked me whether he could paint me. Flattered, I was urged by others to say yes.

The philanthropist and prominent banker, Otto Kahn, had lent the roof garden of his huge town house on upper Fifth

Avenue as a studio for Sorin, who asked me to come every day for several hours to sit.

March 5th

The combination of the Wild Duck, the essay prize, and Sorin's plea to paint me have churned up my insides considerably. I hardly slept at all last night, from sheer burning in the stomach and the brain. I am pleased by the prize, but realize only too well its insignificance. Whereas the Sorin adventure excites me by its romantic, unexpected, dreamlike quality.

March 7th

This Sorin adventure is great, but I know one thing; I work a hell of a sight more than he does. The pose is terrifically exacting; nothing to lean on anywhere, head yanked up and a little on the bias. And I get about three or four rests a morning, which means periods of about ¾ hour gazing steadfast at Savely's Slavic countenance. But he's unconsciously amusing and I'm consciously vain, so I manage to bear up. I think, however, that I'll invest in a straight jacket to support my spine. I'm not as young as I used to be.

• • •

Sorin asked me why I had an expression of extreme sadness, *Weltschmerz*. I told him laughingly that I was born with it. Which is perfectly true. I can't explain it, but I always have been conscious of an undercurrent of vague, impersonal sadness. It may be racial, it may be individual. It is as though I were standing a little apart, and looking at the human struggle with compassionate comprehension. Heaven knows I have no right to feel that way. Heaven knows also it isn't a conscious feeling; but something inseparably bound up with me. In moments of greatest joy I could almost weep; not at the joy, but at something beyond, above, beneath it. I see other things—far off—remote—intangible: and my head is filled with strange music. And the bowed head of my lover is so far, far away; so small.

March 9th

Strange how hard it is to think of anything consecutively while posing. I make up my mind to use every minute of inaction in constructive imagination, yet once I'm on the dais I can no longer follow up an idea than flirt with Sorin. It maddens me, the sheer waste. All this must and undoubtedly will have an influence on my character and works. But I am all for the pleasure of the moment, and it's very hard to sit like a frozen image while a sunny wind blows outside.

I am weary unto death. All I want to do is lie on the grass in the sun and indulge in animal pleasures, among which sleep is the greatest.

• • •

It is strange to me that humans find it impossible to extend the feeling of patriotism from the nation to the race, the race to the universe—and thereby achieve peace. The reason is, I suppose, that patriotism is based not only on love for one's people, but on the spirit of competition, which is always in the end destructive.

Sorin was called back suddenly to Europe, I never knew why. He never finished the picture, although to me it was already a frozen idealization; technically dazzling. I never knew what he did with it.

But more important things were happening. I had met a young man, barely older than me, who had all the qualities most of the contemporaries I met seemed to lack: talent, intelligence, wit, and kindness. He was an artist planning

1. Simon Mannes, itinerant baker in Poland, great-grandfather

2. Helena von Heimburg, singer-grandmother

3. Leopold Damrosch, musician-grandfather

4. Henry Mannes, who brought his family to New York in 1860

5. Nathalia Wittkowska, Henry's wife, my grandmother

6a. David Mannes in his thirties

6b. Early trio

7. David and Clara Mannes in their concert years

8. Clara Damrosch Mannes, mother, musician

9a. David Mannes in his fifties

9b. Summer duet, adagio

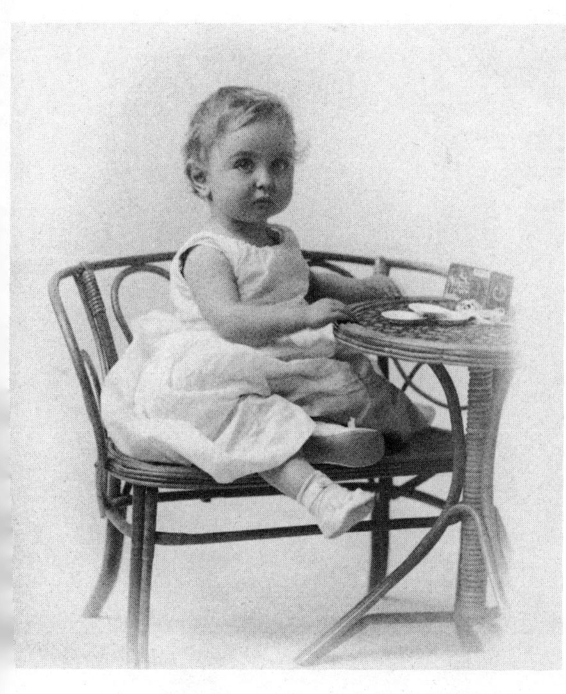

10a. First studio portrait

10b. On stage

11. "She is full of mischief and keeps us all laughing"

12. Life is serious; life is real

13. Twelve or thirteen: irony dawning

14. The graduate

15a. Leopold Damrosch Mannes, mentor, tease

15b. Renaissance youth: my brother

16. Twenty or so, and dreaming

17. M.M. and J.M. – just married

18. Instant sketches by bride in Spain
(Flamenco series)

20. Picador

19. "The seductive wife of our eminent minister"

21. Alfred Cortot, who played in our home while I listened – and drew

22. Girl-about-town

23. Commercial model (Palmolive? Kotex?)

25. The last time I wore ermine

24. Editor doubling as model for Cecil Beaton

26. A gag: Sex in the Thirties

27a. Villa Piazza Calda

27b. M.B. and R.B. – high up

28. Christ 4′ x 5′, by M.M.

29. Restored Madonna in wayside shrine

30. Raoul de Roussy de Sales, late philosopher, journalist – friend

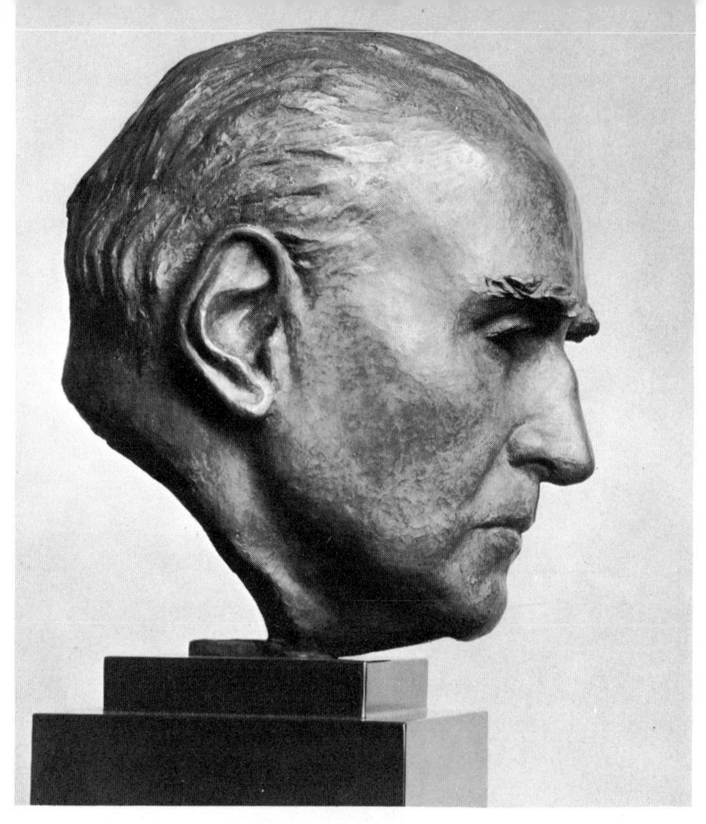

31. My uncle Walter Damrosch

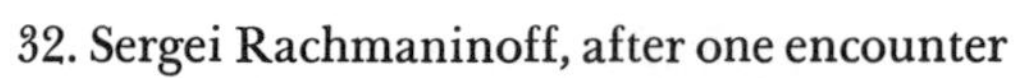

32. Sergei Rachmaninoff, after one encounter

33. M.M. and son

34, 35. Haifa, 1946, the first refugee ships from Europe.

36. Major General Cassel, British commander of the Tel Aviv search and Stern Gang round-up

37. Maxie and me, Berlin, '53

38. The postwar decade: Wife and Writer

39. More lion-mania

to become a scene designer, and his mixture of bloods and backgrounds resembled in many ways my own.

I had not thought of marriage, although that was to come, when the journal suddenly changed tone:

I determined to keep intensely personal thoughts out of these pages, but I'm so much in love, I love so much, that I have to write about it. It's a sublime feeling, and I wallow in it. The wonderful thing is that, though I'm convinced of the deep reality and power and sacredness of this love, I still feel myself a complete and separate identity, capable of independent, abstracted thought and action. I may give myself entirely for the moment and taste the ecstasy of giving, but in the privacy of solitude I belong to no one but myself and my visions. And my visions are those of the creation of immortal beauty.

"Immortal beauty" hardly describes the first play ever to leave my desk for public view. *Foul Is Fair* was a three-act modernization of Macbeth; an ambitious clerk with a more ambitious wife. Yet to see it unfold on stage the summer of 1925 in Woodstock, New York, was for me rhapsodic. Real actors, speaking *my* words before a *real* audience!

If the script still exists, I dare not look: it was probably pretty poor, though some enjoyed it. In any case I prefer to remember the state of levitation that preceded it. And also an incident that accompanied it.

A beautiful tall young man, who reminded me of an Austrian princeling in Metternich's time, hovered nearby in the capacity of producer. He was witty, beguiling, and had a snappy car. I accepted eagerly when he asked me to go on a drive.

We went through the lovely country chattering gaily and,

more and more, personally. Suddenly the car drove up to the verge and stopped.

"Oh damn," he said (or whatever one said), "I'm afraid we've run out of gas."

I believed him, as usual. But when certain designs—isn't that what they once were called?—began to emerge, I pulled away slightly in sudden alarm and said, "I'm sorry, but it's no use. You see, I'm a hermaphrodite."

I had never used the word before, but remembered it from the base of some classic torso of a youth with breasts and a fig leaf.

The worldly princeling darted one terrified glance at me, started the motor, and raced me back to my lodgings.

Whatever romantic inclinations we may have had toward each other were blasted for good. Whenever we met in later years, both of us burst out laughing.

The fact is, I was only partially lying; Wohleben again, suspended between sky and earth, light and dark, free from the gravitational pull: the man in me.

• • •

"Creation of immortal beauty"—indefinitely postponed. By what? Not by lack of effort, surely, or diligence. As for talent, few in a position to judge saw what I wrote, and how could I?

There were no reporters to interview rebellious youth, no television to blow small talents or canny exhibitionists into faddist fame.

As for beauty, which I was told I had in feature and form, this was less help than hindrance to serious work—however tentative—in a world where men were invariably the judges of its worth. In woman beauty was an end in itself. Why reach for more when men reached more for it?

Most men found it hard to take my ambitions seriously. Those who did condescended.

In years to come I often thought what the course of my life would have been if I had been homely, or a man. The attention of men is, to say the least, a marvelous distraction; and loving one can seem more important than anything else—at least for a while. The narcissus in woman goes to the pool too often for reassurance, when the reflection should lie secure in the deep recess of self. This is true of men too, but to a much lesser degree: a chain of alternate pools lie beyond the eyes of a woman.

Besides, I was much too serious: not good at the games people played. Serious not in the sense of dullness or heaviness, more in the dogged search for truth.

This in turn led to a trait not endearing to any society at any time, and certainly not to most men in confrontation with women: candor.

It took me a long while to learn to lie. Not for expedience or betrayal of others. The betrayal was of myself.

But not her younger self, talking to an older man in the "novel":

"What do you want to do most in the world, Jean?"

"Be an influence."

"What do you mean? Everyone's an influence. That old witch over there is an influence—over someone."

"I mean, change things . . . be something that's never been before." She scraped the shadow off with her palette knife, while Peter, brush in hand, looked at her.

"I mean an influence of power . . . and terrific beauty. I want people to worship me, lots of people . . ."

"Have you any idea of how you want to exert that influence?"

"Not yet . . . don't care how . . . guess I'll write." She looked at the grass at her feet, then quickly up at Peter, because she felt his eyes, and grinned.

"Maybe I'll just *be,*" she said.

It was in this year that I read Scott Fitzgerald's *Gatsby* and wrote him in Paris. This was his letter back: in longhand:

Thank you for writing me about Gatsby—I especially appreciate your letter because women, and even intelligent women, haven't generally cared much for it. They do not like women to be presented as *emotionally* passive —as a matter of fact I think most women are, that their minds are taken up with a sort of second-rate and unessential bookkeeping which their apologists call "practicality"—like the French, they are centime-savers in the business of magic. (You see I am a Schopenhauerian, not a Shavian.)

You are thrilled by New York—I doubt you will be after five more years when you are more fully nourished from within. I carry the place around the world in my heart but sometimes try to shake it off in my dreams. America's greatest promise is that something is going to happen, and after a while you get tired of waiting because nothing happens to people except that they grow old, and nothing happens to American art because America is the story of the moon that never rose. Nor does the "minute itself" ever come to life either, the minute not of unrest and hope, but of a glowing peace—such as when the moon rose that night on Gerald and Sara's garden and you said you were happy to be there. No one ever makes things in America with that vast, magnificent, cynical disillusion with which Gerald and Sara make things like their parties.

(They were here, last week, and we spent six or seven happy days together).

My new novel is marvelous. I'm in the first chapter. You may recognize certain things and people in it.

The young people in America are brilliant with second-hand sophistication inherited from their betters of the war generation who to some extent worked things out for themselves. They are brave, shallow, cynical, impatient, turbulent and empty. I like them not. My God, Marya, where are your eyes—are they too fresh and strong to see anything but their own color and contour in the glass? America is so decadent that its brilliant children are damned almost before they are born. Can you name a single American artist except James and Whistler (who lived in England) who didn't die of drink? If it is fresh and strong to be unable to endure or tolerate things-as-they-are, to shut your eyes or to distort and lie—then you're right, Marya Mannes, and no one has ever so misinterpreted the flowers of civilization, the Greek and Gallic idea, as

Your sincere admirer,
F. Scott Fitzgerald

In public, and more out of exhilaration than self-advertisement, I have always been an exhibitionist, tossing out freely fragments of myself. But the core I learned to hide except for the very few men who were strong enough to face it and even accept it.

Otherwise I blunted the edge of my intelligence for fear it would cut. I learned to speak lightly of dreams and with a graceful deprecation of gifts, such as they were. The approval of men was paramount, and who of them wanted an independent soul?

One of them was the young man I soon married. And he paid for it dearly.

• • •

4.

The hour before my wedding I was in my room in the family apartment, dressed as a bride and crying in my father's arms.

Not unusual, I was told. But details of my wedding certainly were, for those times. Hating accepted ritual, I had refused both veil and ring, seeing in them seals of bondage. I wore instead a long white empire satin dress with a square neck and a wreath of gardenias on my head.

I was going to marry the person I wanted to live with and suddenly I was overcome with a sadness so immense that it burst all bounds.

By the time I had walked with my family the one block to the place of the wedding (never church: the small auditorium of their music school) I had composed myself well enough.

The music was lovely, the groom and his family looked

very dear, and my father's arm hooked itself tightly into mine. Only my fingers holding a cluster of white flowers trembled.

A minister-friend spoke the words, there was joy and gaiety and champagne afterward, and my husband and I were off on a wave of happiness first to the old Brevoort Hotel for the night, then to a boat to take us to Spain and France.

• • •

It will serve no purpose in the course of this odyssey to embarrass the three men who have been my husbands, all of them living. Each has given me much in different ways, two of them are still friends.

Failure in marriage is never a single fault, and the failures of mine are attributable as much to the demands of marriage itself as to the natures of those involved.

I have come to believe, however, that there are some people—men and women alike—who should not be married at all. Individuals too complex to handle a second complexity in daily enclosure; too singular to overlap; too emotionally and sexually greedy for one partner.

To live together as long as mutual trust and affection and—most especially—communication exist, yes. To assume the years of responsibility for children involved, yes. But not, for many of us, as the essential role.

And not, certainly, for a woman who has been—for want of a better phrase—a spiritual hermaphrodite all her life without acknowledging it until too late.

At twenty-one, certainly, I was in no way equipped to be a wife, let alone a mistress. In my journal I might write that "I may give myself entirely for the moment and taste the ecstasy of giving," but I had still no knowledge of real surrender.

The emotions I felt had always outpaced the slow-developing body, the female core had still not silenced the racing mind or submerged the will. Something in me refused to open up or be opened, much as I longed for union and release.

(Wohleben prods: haven't you forgotten something about that ghost? The fear of children?)

Ah yes, the fear. Allayed by the common agreement that we were too young to have them and could not afford them.

But then, not to have them meant a golden wishbone thrust in the vital tissues. (She could not blame men for not wanting to sheath themselves.) But her spirit rejected it even if the flesh didn't. It was an alien substance: something wrong (to her). The resistance against it was a double contraction. But ignorance forced acceptance of pain that need not have been, and guilt.

That ghost thought it was all her fault, and pled for change. When it came, through a stranger, she destroyed the marriage.

• • •

Yet at the same time life was opening up. We loved and admired each other as human beings, we were avid for new experiences. Our six months abroad was a happy prelude to three more years of companionship and work: his in painting and theater, my own in new ways of expression.

In writing there was, at last, a loosening up and a turning outward. All the new things I saw demanded new cadences, finally out of context of self, and into the world.

A few, never printed, of course, follow as evidence of

this search. A long visit to the cathedral of Toledo, suffused with El Greco's vision, spurred these notes:

But the little boys, the tiny little boys clatter across the dark stones in vermilion and lace, holding gold and silver crosses, swinging big silver incense pots, swinging them past the nose of the little shrouded girl and leaving her in a scented cloud. Their small heads are as clipped and shiny and brown-black as the flanks of a fine horse. And they clatter and scuffle casually through the formal gloom, splashing the floor with red, and swinging censers.

Mass is beginning. Priests come from everywhere. Priests come from the cloisters, the sacristy, the capitulary halls; from the canonical hall and the crypt. Priests come, red robes swinging around their measured footsteps, finest lace falling on round abdomens. Little red hats, little black hats with bright green pompoms set on austere or stupid or voluptuous heads; on sad or benign or pompous heads. Old gates and old doors clang with the coming of the many priests and their little red splashes of boys running between and around and ahead of them like pilot fish among whales.

They settle themselves in the gorgeous stalls of the choir, the priests. Spreading their crimson skirts, they take their accustomed places, each in his own carved cubicle. One priest, just before curtsying at the choir entrance, darts hot black eyes at a beautiful woman, who reflects the heat, fixing him with her gaze, lingering on falling red and falling lace and heavy mouth. But he turns insolently, bends a knee and swishes through into the stalls.

Christ, tortured, hangs his head a hundred feet above the throne of the cardinal, a hundred feet of intricate gold and wood. He hangs his dark head in the dark vault, and his pale limbs stretch down.

A rustle: the priests bend down for their prayer books. A canon rests his soft hand, with one jewel, on the arm of his stall. The chanting begins. A loud blurred monotone, insistent. Only one voice rises in beauty, mellow and resonant. It is the voice of the canon with a jewel on his hand. One voice is cold and harsh, the voice of the priest with the hot black eyes. The sound is balanced levelly in the air, and never let drop. There is exaltation in the intense control of sound. But the steadiness is sinister.

Out of the loud drone suddenly tears a high piercing puerile voice, like a tin spear ripping maroon plush. It comes from the wide mouth of one of the little scarlet boys—a cataclysmic shriek, lasting a moment. But every five minutes it rends and pierces again the drone of the priests. And when it is over, the little boy grins, showing a gap in his teeth.

The Silencer stands outside the grills of the choir, the soaring grills, the slender bars shooting up into iron leafage. He is an ancient man in a black dusty cloak and a white wig, askew. But his staff is five feet of heavy silver, heavily carved, and he stamps it with pride. He stamps it that no one may stare into the holy of holies and stand before Christ. The weight of the silver staff is almost too much for the Silencer to bear, but he pounds it with pride.

The mass never stops. The insistent drone seems to increase, to swell into a magnificent roar of men. The red silk cloaks of the priests glow in the stalls like separate setting suns. The puerile cry rises higher every time. It has almost struck the thorns on the dark head of Christ.

A week later a traveling circus in a small French town burned itself on my eyes and mind:

Scarlet the circus wagons and gilt, and red lions roar. And Director Bracciotti is fed on Chianti and pink pork. And the seven children Bracciotti are white and wan; wan and wanting a mother. Their tights are holey.

"Allez-oup!" Thin thing, the youngest, in streaked cyclamen tights, rises on sticklike arm on the hands of her father Bracciotti. "Smile at Pappa!" shouts Bracciotti. The thin thing stretches her impoverished mouth. "Allez-oup!" (Bracciotti, laughing.) Down jumps the wizened, noiseless, pointing her toes on sawdust. "I kiss you!" quavers the mouth, and thin arms arabesque. (Kisses are blown into the smoke.) "Allez-oup!"

Crack of the whip, Pit-Pit the clown grimaces, breathing obscenity from a rubber mouth. Turns somersaults. Nine little curs run out, in bonnets. "Hoop-la!" cries Pit-Pit. Little mongrels skip to little chairs and sit. "Hoop-la!" squeaks Pit-Pit.

Interlude, little dog drags pot from cabinet and sits.

Cages brought on, and stench. In the smoky yellow a hyena drags its nethers on the ocher dust, snarling. Foam from its hydrophobial maw, and round eyes lightless. "Allez-oup!" La Palina! Woman in scarlet and yellow shawl in the cage, snarling "Carramba, marrumba, brrraaa-aaaccia!" cracking her whip across the hyena's froth, frothing. Woman with hydrophobial maw and scarlet hyena snarling and stinking in the ocher smoke. "Allez-oup!"

Second Bracciotti, a boy with a head by Theotocopuli the Greek, springs in the glare. Long tights of rose washed into grayness hanging on length. ("Hoop-la!" roars genial father.) Blanching, the boy swings up to trapeze, and rose tights fade in the dusk of the tent peak, but the face shines, sweating. He turns and turns and turns, wheeling. "Allez-oup!" he cries, and drops to the sawdust. Long arms wave kisses to the mob, and Bracciotti grins. "Allez-oup!" says he.

Then, with the blare of brass, the clowns. Clowns and clowns, all rubber-mouthed with shoe-button eyes, and crackling. Cartwheels and squealing and Bracciotti cracking his whip at their heels. "Hoop-la! Hoop-la!" Around and around and around, jumping and rolling. Behind chalk-whiteness and the button eyes, the paler of six of the Bracciotti lies, the motherless. "Allez-oup!" cries old Bracciotti. The clowns arise and describe grotesqueries in the smoky glare, bowing. "They kiss you, they kiss you!" roars crimson-coated father.

Scarlet the circus wagons and gold, and red lions roar. And Director Bracciotti is fed on Chianti and pink pork. But the seven children Bracciotti are white and wan—warmed by the love of a red-shawled, laughing hyena.

In southern Spain, my first bullfight enthralled and sickened me:

The black hulk hurls,
Buries his terrible horns in the horse's belly,
All the way in.
And jabs and jabs and jabs and jabs again
And pins the nag and its rider against the wall
and then withdraws with dark red dripping horns,
and a wound in its withers like a well of blood,
and lolling tongue. . . .

• • •

The nag has clattered to the ground, but boys in red
Whip it again to its feet with little sticks,

Whip it up, and then it runs
around and around the arena without a sound
in quite an ordinary measured gallop,
its vitals swinging further and further from the wound,
Slapping the ground. . . .
    The horse then follows its entrails to the earth,
    And red boys cover the massacre
    with burlap shrouds.

. . .

    Silence.
Standing a little back, the espada smiles,
Watching
The bull's mouth opens and coughingly
a red flood pours.
    Silence.
The great black beast
Totters a little, sways, reels,
Drops.
Kicks once and dies on the passionless sand.

. . .

Nothing important; but a craft was beginning.

Barring a translation of Mallarmé's *L'Après-Midi d'un Faune* printed in the program notes of the New York Philharmonic, my first professional publication was in a magazine called *Creative Art*. Rockwell Kent, who first edited it, asked me to write gallery notes for it in the flattering assumption that I knew something about art if only through exposure to it.

Later Lee Simonson, the distinguished stage designer, became editor and suggested I contribute to a column called News of the Month.

A sample of my new-found pomposity can be found in these 1927 remarks spurred by exhibitions of Burchfield and Peggy Bacon, among others:

> Irony is almost always a sign of maturity. In a nation as well as in a man it marks the death of adolescence and the birth of consciousness. It is gratifying, therefore, to find this irony, this satiric comment, creeping into American art; and, what is better still, giving it a beauty and a poignance that naïveté seldom achieves.
>
> . . .
>
> However, I must dissipate any impression that irony is a necessary part of art, or to be exalted for its own sake. Perhaps the greatest paintings in the world are free of it. For it implies a certain sense of superiority of the artist over his subject. It implies either an amused tolerance, or contempt, or utter condemnation. And the Giottos, Grecos, and Rembrandts of this life seem void of that.

At the end of the column, this footnote after Picabia:

> The clearer the medium of expression the bigger must be the idea expressed; whereas a complicated and abstruse technique can get along for a while on a very small, very shallow idea. But it is a habit of the intelligentsia to exalt complexity and scorn clarity, to see strength in chaos and banality in coherence.

The developing passion by then, however, was theater. With Eugene O'Neill and the Provincetown Playhouse holding stage-center, with my husband designing sets for Broadway productions, with a growing circle of actor, producer, and director friends, drama became my favorite outlet for writing.

Two of my own scripts were bought by Broadway producers, and one was performed in the fall of 1930.

Called *Cafe,* it concerned expatriates in Paris, rootlessness and conflicting loves.

It was a monumental flop and closed in four days. One critic of blessed memory (he is dead) suggested I had Chekhovian qualities that merited watching. The opinion of others was best expressed by another who advised that "Miss Mannes should go back to whatever she was doing before."

The fact that the supporting actress got drunk on opening night and transposed dialogue meant for the last act into the first, may not have helped. I only know that the playwright passed out deliberately after the first-night party and wept every morning for six weeks thereafter.

The phoenix being sturdy, however, rose; to fall again later—a recurring pattern.

• • •

One play that was never produced but clearly belongs in this chronicle of a social rebel, follows:

The First Woman
A Play in One Act

The scene is the small refectory of the Monastery of Mount Labos in Siberia. As the curtain rises five monks are seated at the table, eating, drinking, and discussing. The youngest, Geronimus, is flushed with drink and speaks with passion. Paul is fat and benign, Christopher, emaciated,

Martin, big-nosed and dominant, and Brother John, young, gentle, and inspired.

Geronimus

Why do we always speak of women when we never see them—why?

Paul

Precisely because we never see them, Brother Geronimus.

Christopher

It is better to speak of mysteries than of facts. Only one thing can be said of a fact, but one can speak of mysteries through a long night—through many nights—.

John

They are all Virgin Marys. They are all virginal, are women.

Geronimus

And was that virginal that in my infancy gave me to drink and warmed me with such overwhelming sultriness that I stifled?

John

Ay, virginal. Mary gave her son, Jesus, milk and warmed him in the cold stable.

Paul

Ah, to be torn from that with eyes still blind from birth and reaching mouth—!

Geronimus

And dragged to this bleakness, among bleak men.

John

There is no bleakness here—

Paul

Wine be praised.

Geronimus

(Excited)

We call all women Virgin Marys because Our Lady is all we know of the race that is not men. The reverent Founder of this holy order took care that no other mention be in the Bible!

Paul

Yes, one can see where passages are torn from the Holy Book and obliterated.

Christopher

It is as well. Our Founder was a holy of holies and would extirpate evil where he saw it.

Geronimus

It seems we are the only order finding evil in the Book of Books!

Martin

Who told you that? What do you know of other orders, guarded from birth to death on this alien peak?

Geronimus

(Sullen)

Mind your own business, Martin.

Paul

The boy may have heard from our late Brother Ignatius, who joined the order at the age of seven. As you know, he was a dwarf, and at seven looked like a puling baby.

John

At seven I understood much—

Christopher

Brother Geronimus, I, too, have memories like yours, smothered in mist. But the holy being that bore me seemed immense as a cloud and as cool and as white. And I remember the tearing from her and then the impersonal cold.

John

Tell me, Brother Martin, I never knew—how did they gather new souls to grow into monks when no one may leave the monastery living?

Martin

The Holy Marys that bore us took us here. They know that there is no life so sacred as the life on Labos. But only the greatest have the strength to do it. They carry their infant alone from the valley up those ten thousand feet to the gate of the monastery. There is a cradle of rocks outside the gate. She lays the child on the cradle and with all the power left in her body lifts up her voice to the sky and cries: "Mater dolorosa e beata sum!"

John

I heard that on the wind once at sundown—a terrible sound, full of agony.

Martin

It comes from agony. Then our ancient and most venerable brother, hearing this, opens the gate (he is gatekeeper) and takes the infant in—and closes the gate.

John

Ah, now I see why there are years when no new souls arrive—and years with only one, or two—

Geronimus

(With a sneer)

And, has no holy mother ever stayed to see what happened to her child? And has no venerable and ancient brother caught her there—within the gates?

Christopher

O blasphemy, Geronimus, rotten blasphemy!

Martin

(Sternly)

You know youself that every monk in this order must lose his eyes when he is sixty.

Geronimus

Eyes are not all.

Christopher

No, Brother Geronimus, but the mother who is strong enough to bring her child up the mountain and forsake it is strong enough to turn away when the gate opens. She knows she will be accursed if she approaches.

Paul

Once though, a hundred years ago maybe, a blessed Mary tried to force her way in the monastery walls to retrieve her child. The blind brother had to push her out. He was frail, but she only struggled a moment. They say—they say he spoke of her as soft—as soft and warm he spoke of her, the Virgin Mother.

Martin

Enough, Brother Paul!

John

(Dreaming)

And one must wait till sixty for eternal peace—?

Geronimus

(Irritated)

O you old dotard, sighing for infirmity!

Christopher

Geronimus, each sense is an infirmity. We were better without.

John

The strength of these Marys, our mothers, to sacrifice the fruit of their boughs!

Geronimus

I have another question, Brothers! not prompted by wine or malice. Listen now—if these mothers of ours, these Virgin Marys, these women—if they are so infinitely holy, so blessed —why are they shut forever from our sight. Couldn't they help us in our work, as Mary herself helps us?

(Long Pause)

Martin

(Scowling)

Your mind rattles with restlessness—

John

No—answer him, answer him!

Paul

No, don't. Every answer brings a question and questions bring discomfort.

Christopher

Geronimus: we are the chosen. It is so written in the Bible. Being the chosen and being formed in the image of God, we are enough in ourselves. The world with all its evil and its good is in us. There is only one Mary, the Mother of Christ, and she is all we need. These women below in the valleys of the world are but fleshy reflections of this first Spirit—and created for the aid of our weaker brothers.

Geronimus

(Rising, unappeased)

Agh, you all know so much! Then tell me, how am I strong because I happen to have been laid on a stone by my mother and reared on the heights instead of in the valleys? "Weaker brothers"!

(Goes out)

Martin

Brother Geronimus is not well.

Paul

Too thin. The heat compresses him, the cold pierces him. Look at me, did I ever doubt?

Christopher

We all should doubt—but not with certainty. We should doubt doubtfully, else it is not doubt but assertion.

Paul

Pickle pickle, pockle pockle, pickle pickle.

Martin

Are you ill too?

Paul

Nothing, only whenever Christopher philosophizes it sounds like that.

Christopher

(Smiling)

To you. Thought depresses you, reason compresses you!

John

(With immense reverence)

You are wonderful, Brother Christopher.

Christopher

Ay, wonderful—full of wonder, John.

(Suddenly a Woman appears in the arched refectory entrance—a coarse vulgar-moving peasant woman, heavy with child and slightly drunk. Brazenly she stands there while the Brothers gaze at her in ineffable wonder, struck suddenly dumb)

(High and ecstatic)

Ave Maria Sanctissima!

John

(Sinking low)

O holy holy—O Mother of God.

Martin

(Aghast)

Ave Maria Beatissima!

Paul

(Kneeling)

O thou divine, O thou Blessed Virgin of God!

Woman

(Amazed)

Lord! Is that the way you feel? Get up, sillies.

Christopher

O cover your faces, Brothers, before the light that is vouchsafed us.

John

I cover my face.

Martin

Ave Maria Purissima—

Paul

(Murmuring)

Sanctus—sanctus—sanctus—.

Woman

Listen, get up, get up, all of you—

Martin

(Rising)

Rise, Brothers, if the Virgin bid you.

Woman

Virgin? Ha, virgin you said?

Christopher

O holy, holy, holy.

Paul

That this should happen in my life—!

John

O Holy Mother of the Lamb!

(Loud tapping of a staff on stones)

Anselm

(Invisible)

O woe—O woe, Brothers!!!

(The ancient and venerable Anselm enters, blind distraught, and trembling)

O Brothers, where is she, where has she gone, Brothers?

Martin

Hush, Brother Anselm, and bow to the Holy Mother of Christ!

John

Ave Maria Sanctissima—

Anselm

Ah Brothers, Brothers, I heard her voice, I heard her "Mater dolorosa e beata sum!" and I went to the gate and opened it, but there was no infant on the stone, only this woman passing me—passing me in flight, with the rustle of wings! O woe!

Martin

Anselm, lament not! This is a holy visitation of the first and the most blessed Virgin Mary. Bow down!

Christopher

How like the Mother of Christ to stand submissive at the portal, waiting and crying to be let in!

Paul

That this should happen in my life—

John

With the rustle of wings she came, like an angel!

Anselm

(Weakly)

Ave Maria Sanctissima—

Woman

And now, by the Lord, she's hungry as a hog. Have you no food?

Martin

Paul, give her wine and bread. Quick!

Woman

No, I want the young'un to give me food. The little girlish one! (points to John)

Martin

Quick, John, serve Our Lady of Sorrows, serve her!

(John, trembling with exaltation, pours wine into a tankard and puts a slice of bread on a plate)

Woman

(Grinning)

Our Lady of Sorrows is right, Brothers! Kicked out of the house by a drunken sot, and *that* seven months with child in the belly—

Christopher

(Whispering)

O blessed day! Brothers, the Lord Christ is in her womb!

Paul

Christ to be born again—O holy, holy!

John

(Approaching her with the food and kneeling)

Here—here is food, blessed Virgin—

Woman

(Taking it from him and immediately munching and drinking)

Thanks, white face. Only stop this virgin business, it's ridiculous.

(Goes to the chair Christopher has vacated and sits in it)

For the love of Christ, sit down. You make me nervous.

(They all sit, slowly, lost in wonder at this divine manifestation)

The wine is good.

Paul

I am overwhelmed, Blessed Mary, with my own feet I trampled—

Martin

Paul is our horn of plenty—

Woman

In fact, if you give me more, I'll tell the story of my life. It's beautiful—

John

(Rushing to her with wine, kneeling again)

Here—Blessed Lady—here—

Woman

(Taking it)

Well, I was born of poor but well-meaning parents—

Christopher

Of lowly parents was she born—

Woman

The night I was born, the roof leaked—badly—and my father swore at the village carpenter.

Paul

In a storm was she born!

John

(With wonder)

In a storm!

Woman

Before I was fourteen you men came rushing around me, begging for a look—

Martin

At fourteen, Brothers, she cast her blessed spell!

Paul

Ah, Purissima!

Woman

But I wouldn't give 'em my little finger, they were all as poor as my parents. I wanted a castle.

Martin

So young, Brothers, so young and already spurning the base for the lofty, the poor of spirit for the great!

Woman

Of course, I took pity on a few of the simpletons. I had to, in self-defense, and then it's unholy to be a spinster—at least, down in the valley.

Christopher

Listen, Brothers, to Our Lady, she stopped to solace the simple of mind and was full of pity!

John

Mary the Pitiful, Mother of the Lamb—

Woman

Well then, a husky ruffian with a stiff beard came into the valley—a workman, but he had a way with him, and this time I flopped. I flopped heavily.

Paul

(Whispering)

Brothers, is this Joseph she speaks of? It must be Joseph—

Woman

I don't remember his name, perhaps it's Joseph, but stop interrupting this beautiful story of myself. Well, anyway, I was crazy—I must have been crazy—and got myself with child. Funny to have a child without a father, huh? What is it you call it, there's a name for it—

Martin

The Immaculate Conception, to the glory of God and His angels!

John

Ah beatissima Maria!

Woman

The what?

Christopher

(Softly with tenderness)

The Immaculate Conception, Blessed Virgin—

Woman

Naw, *bastard,* sillies, *bastard!* That's what I've got unless Joseph stops drinking and sees his duty!

Paul

(Smiling benignly)

Ah the simplicity of Our Lady, Brothers, the divine simplicity of the Queen of Heaven!

Martin

Bow to the Holy Bastard, Brothers, the Virgin wishes the Lord Jesus so to be called!

Paul

(Raising his hands aloft)

O Bastard Divinity! O Holy Bastard of God!

Woman

What I don't understand is: are you crazy before you get here or does this life make you crazy? I suppose it makes you crazy, you haven't much time to be insane before you come here—!

John

(Low)

Martin, I do not understand Our Lady—

Martin

Who of us can understand Holiness when it speaks? Listen, John, with your spirit and not with your brain.

Woman

Well, now do you want to know why I came here? Do you, you madmen?

(They all lean forward, tense and adoring. She slaps her stomach coarsely)

It's this, holy Brothers, this thing here that brought me up your accursed mountain! They say the greatest life a son can have is to be a monk on Labos. Well then, let him have it, he'll be the first to be great in our rotting family! I know it's a boy, the village witch told me so—what do I want with him, what do I want with a child without a father? So I've come to bear him in your monastery, Brothers.

Christopher

O beatissimi fratres, God has descended in our unworthy midst!

John

(Almost inaudible)

Brothers—are we to witness the birth of Christ, then?

Martin

Hush, John! It is too unbreathably holy to think of!

Woman

I figured the boy would know even less of women and mothers and the dirty world if he was born in your midst, instead of down in the valley—that he'd be that much holier with a monkish midwife!

(Laughs and rises groggily to her feet)

And d'you know a joke? D'you know a wonderful joke? I'm going to call the little bastard Jesus!

(A dead silence. Geronimus, wild-eyed, suddenly appears in the dark background, staring at the woman, but unseen by the rest. The Brothers, of one accord, sink to their knees on the ground, join their hands in prayer, and burst forth in a canticle of holy joy, a soaring and bursting chorus of exaltation in Latin. As they sing, Geronimus slowly approaches the woman, feverish with discovery. And just as the chorus reaches its climax of impassioned purity, he touches her lightly and fearfully on the arm, as if he touched fire.)

CURTAIN

Unplayable, of course. And unthinkable, then. Yet during the next few years, two more full-length plays were sold to Broadway producers—one called *The Strad Mystery,* about the theft of a violin, the other a collaboration with Worthington Miner about Rasputin. Bad luck dogged both, for different reasons. In the case of Rasputin, bought by Jed Harris, the actor chosen for the lead part died ten days before the planned rehearsals.

Strange as it may seem, in fact, for most of us working in theater and writing and music, depression memories center less on breadlines and suicides than on productive days and speak-easy nights. The reason for this was not only the political and social immaturity of so many of us. It was partly that our families and our friends never had any money to invest, never dealt in the stock market, and somehow managed to survive without a marked difference in our way of living. Not trained from infancy to be consumers, we were brought up to buy only what we needed and could afford. And even these needs could be whittled down in crisis.

So although those older and wiser and less fortunate felt a creeping desolate fear for the country, and although the sight of men who looked like teachers or bankers or lawyers selling apples on street corners made us hurry by, chilled, we were not much changed. Through it all, somehow, I never knew why—music was played, theaters were full, books were published—and the speak-easies flourished. Tony's on Fifty-second Street was crowded every night with writers and actors and dancers and playwrights who could still buy drinks and make fun of themselves. And the WPA was the life line of many who couldn't, especially artists. There was a sense of profound common humanity in that Depression to which the current slump bears no resemblance at all, being cold at the core.

This common humanity in the face of Prohibition, moreover, made lawbreakers of us all. My favorite instance of this defiance was the sight of my parents making gin in the bathroom and the sound of my mother calling Professor Robert W. Wood, our long-time physicist friend, in Baltimore and asking "Robert—just what proportion of juniper do you use in yours?"

• • •

Not only nostalgia made the theater of those years seem effulgent. It ranged from Eugene O'Neill's *Mourning Becomes Electra* to George Gershwin's *Girl Crazy* with Ethel Merman's debut. It included Maxwell Anderson's *Elizabeth the Queen* and Marc Connelly's *The Green Pastures;* Noel Coward's *Private Lives* and Philip Barry's *Hotel Universe:*

European kitsch (of a high order) could be sampled in Molnar's *Reunion in Vienna,* with Lunt and Fontanne; American comedy in Ring Lardner's and George S. Kaufman's *June Moon.*

None of these had greatness, few of them would survive exposure today. But they brought to their audiences a kind of civilized or festive or comic pleasure which, to me, seems in very short order now.

In any event, contiguity played a large part in my delight. Since my husband was increasingly involved in production, I, too, was drawn into the circle of light that suffused the stage and the people who created for it and performed in it.

Eugene O'Neill was, of course, the pervasive dramatic presence, and although I never met him, his plays went deeply under my skin, brooded over my dreams.

The more I saw of the theater then, the more I became drunk with its possibilities, spellbound by people like Robert Edmond Jones, the designer and great friend, and Alfred and Lynn Fontanne, for whose production of Molnar's *The Guardsmen* my young husband had designed the sets. What so enchanted my father at fourteen now held me in thrall in my twenties: the voices, the looks, the talents of theater people, the smell of theater itself.

How much more beautiful and gay than musicians! (the child-ghost thought). And so kind, so generous! Once when we went backstage after a performance to the star-couple's dressing room, Lynn Fontanne made a special fuss about me. She took my face in her hands and turned it this way and that, laughing a little.

And then she said, "Sit down a minute, my dear," and she took her eye pencil and drew a line over my eyelashes very deftly and then said, "There! You must always do that, my dear. Now you are perfect!"

I left, trailing glory.

Those theater years spoiled me, in a way. There has been wonderful theater since, but something has gone. Not talent, certainly; rather an ambience created as much by spectators as by creators. For one thing, performers and audience shared common standards of professionalism. Diction and literacy, whether in low comedy or high drama, were basic demands, wit an asset, meaning essential in any serious play. These transcended the inevitable and necessary changes in attitudes, styles, thoughts, and techniques that time always brings.

There was plenty to harrow and shock on stage, as well as amuse, even then. But communication was not confrontation, self-expression was not self-indulgence, and no playwright could hope to hold his audience by abuse and tedium merely to make his point.

His point was to create, through the force of his own imagination, the illusion of reality and the reality of illusion: a force, if he knew his job, that no proscenium, no physical separation between stage and audience could impede.

The current assumption that physical involvement between actor and spectator heightens feeling is one of several convenient crutches for failure in craft as well as in imagination. There is no "People's Theater" any more than there is "People's Art." Both sustain the myth, tenderly cherished, that everybody is as good as everybody else, and that there is such a thing as group creation.

I speak now as a member of the audience, saluting my betters when they appear in the full realization that my own efforts in theater warranted, in themselves, a proper humility.

Cafe was certainly no adornment to the theater of the thirties, and although I finally managed to have some sketches in a successful revue called *The Little Show,* my theatrical "career" could be best described as "How Not to Succeed by Really Trying."

• • •

By 1931 I had left my husband to continue an intense and tempestuous affair with a brilliant Catalan, a biologist at the Rockefeller Institute. I moved to a small apartment in the East Fifties, taking only my desk and my upright piano among other family objects, and subsisting on what I could earn together with what my parents could afford to add. I had at least the minimal decency to refuse alimony from a man whom I had deeply, if unwillingly, hurt.

Once installed I began to experience the extraordinary sense of freedom which characterized the two long intervals between marriages and should have taught me something about myself. Freedom to roam, both inwardly and outwardly, to explore, to risk, and ultimately to know a variety of loves with men: what was wrong with this life?

I did not then—and do not now—understand the term "promiscuous": used perjoratively, of course, and only of women. What was wrong with giving and receiving warmth, pleasure, affection, and release even if these could not qualify as love? If it was not wrong for men (Oh yes, philanderer, rake, swordsman, what have you—all implicitly more flattering than diminishing) why was it wrong for women? One at a time, to be sure. For one night, or ten, or two years. But how could you know a man you liked without knowing his body?

Of course you accepted the consequences of these acts. You accepted uncertainty, disappointment, pain, loneliness, and insecurity. But you lived as fully as you could, and often as deeply.

Money was hard to come by, but men were generous with meals on the town, and in between I joined my parents for dinner or scrounged on friends. Somehow—God knows how—my translations, reviews for the New Republic, an odd piece or two, and an option on one more play that never saw light paid for the rent and what clothes I needed beyond those I already owned. Again, no consumer economy to spur discontent and escalate new wants.

More important, to me at least, was that the writing seemed to broaden, grow innovative and more complex. Wohleben and many others were being conceived in a new book I had then begun, of which these are some opening pages:

PART I

This book is founded on an obsession: the old, human obsession of relating things apparently unrelated; of finding a fundamental pattern; of wrenching order out of primal chaos.

If you believe this order is possible, then you must also believe that chaos, ultimately, does not exist. There is only our blindness; our bewilderment; our defeat in face of the enormous wealth of life. For this air, at this moment, hold everything that ever was, that is, or that ever will be. We are overwhelmed by a constant, imminent totality; are able—the most acute of us—to grasp only one-thousandth part of it; and call the rest, the unfilchable, chaos.

Everything, every movement of fingers or turn of leaf in the wind, means something; is important in the fact of its being. That is significance enough; this affirmation of life.

The obsession in pattern, in the relating of leaf to finger, of voice in the street to shadow on the floor, must resolve itself into several and separate obsessions in leaf and finger, in voice and in shadow. Must, and does lead to an exultance in Fact; to an intense study of it, and compassion for it. Compassion, for there is no understanding without an impersonal pity for its existence; without a deep humility before the mystery it is born from and returns to.

If, then, one is able to see clearly and with compassion each separate thing, each fact, each infinitesimal movement of living, the chaos will begin to dissolve, and the form stand forth in awful and absolute purity.

This book then, in an atomic way, is an attempt to do this. It is a voyage of discovery in the world of fact. There will be no plot, no single story, no suspense, no climax, and no conclusion. I do not know what will happen to the next three hundred pages. I shall merely choose, out of an infinity of them, those facts which move me most to study and compassion; shall set them down, as they occur to me, and see what happens. I believe now that a logical and natural growth will happen. There will be an evolution, at first imperceptible, later clearer, until it reaches a pitch and an intensity that no forced growth or maneuvered artifice could bear. There will be design —great and simple and all-embracing. And if its boundaries be at first invisible, that is no proof of their nonexistence. There is a point at which sound, being too high or too low, becomes inaudible; at which light, shivering too quickly or too slowly, cannot be seen. The limits of the universe are the limits of our understanding.

This, then, is the book: an absorption, a series of

absorptions, in the Thing. And if experimentation bores you, or if you are too much of a skeptic to embark on as mad and indefinite a quest as this must seem, no one will force you to join me. There are, happily for you, a legion of writers who can give you all the sequence and definition you crave for; who lay the stencil of their limitations over the world of matter and, by ignoring whatever the solid part of their stencil covers, achieve a very satisfying pattern.

I not only do not know what will happen in the next three hundred pages; I do not know what form it will take—prose, poetry, essay, novel, play. Whatever passage demands poetry shall be written in poetry. Whatever dialogue suggests theater will be written as theater. I believe, firmly, that matter should control form, that surface is determined by the volume beneath it. I have seen sculptors who use the same stone and the same chisels to carve the heads of an old politician and a little girl, violinists who play dissonances sweetly; painters who paint flesh as they would paint trees; novelists who put words of the same color and rhythm in the mouths of all their characters. And I call these artists limited and inaccurate. There are themes that demand the mellowness of an oboe, others that cry for a violin's acidity. Let the themes be satisfied.

There are those of you who may say that a creator should have complete control over his matter. That it is my duty to know the beginning, the middle, and the end of this book, even if I choose to keep that knowledge to myself. I can only reply to that: if I control each moment of writing, as I hope to do, then of necessity I control the whole. That is mathematically sound.

You may say, then, that there should be unity in a work of art: how can there be unity in a collection of facts? To this I say: the fact that I, an entity, relate these disunited things is unity enough. Have you noticed the miracle of a mirror? Put any collections of objects in front of it, and the glass will draw them together, give them the homogeneity of its reflection. The dullest mirror will do that.

Above all, more than anything, I want to communicate the excitement of Fact: what the eye sees, what the ear hears, what the hands touch and the nose smells. Transpose all the "The's" in that sentence to "my's," and you see how the objective and the subjective are unified in fact; that fact is, and contains, all experience. It is the privilege of living to be aware of a curtain's fold or the intonation of a human voice. To be acutely, agonizingly conscious of the moment that is always present and always passing. To this excitement, to this awareness, to the beauty of words and to a boundless longing for discovery—this book, then, is given over.

II

In his research laboratory, the young biologist Haley was examining some rabbits he had injected with different vira. There were six tiers of cages lining the room, and in each cage a rabbit palpitating, in a trance of fear or the state beyond fear. Their sides were shorn, were red skin raw with punctures and lesions. Haley lifted one, a big gray one, out of its cage. Both sides were hideous with varicolored boils, and a gleam of pleasure warmed Haley's eyes.

"Look at this," he called to his assistant, a young Swede. The Swede came over and followed Haley's pointing to an enormous scarlet lesion on the gray rabbit. "Plenty of enhancement there, all right—"

"Yes—fine—"

Haley put the quivering rabbit back in its cage, walked over to a row of glass jars with white mice in them.

"I can't understand what's keeping the tumor on No. 6 down," he said, as he took a mouse out by its tail and looked at a small hard blister on the belly.

"Three months already, is it not?" asked the assistant.

"More. Oh, this is a long game, Jensen. There's no end to it." He sighed, his square face and his small brown eyes sad for a moment. "Think you're getting somewhere, then something goes wrong and you have to start all over again."

"To hell with you," he said to the mouse and dropped it back into the jar. Then he went to his desk and wrote things down, slowly, his forehead grooved with perplexity.

Jensen looked at him as a spaniel looks at his master; then went to the next room to sterilize syringes. That night he wrote to his mother in Gothenburg: "I am very lucky to be working with Haley. He's an extraordinary man, really the best in his field—

"He never shows anything. They say his mother, whom he adored, died three days ago, but he never told anyone about it. Just keeps right on, like a bricklayer laying one brick after another. Anyway, I'm glad if I can be the mortar. It will be a fine building."

In a laboratory in Moscow, monkeys injected with paralysis virus could not understand why their legs failed to move. They crouched, small and helpless in the backs of their cages, eyes like black beads, brows wrinkled, lips chattering with fright.

One of them, only partially paralyzed, kept plucking at his stiff leg, pushing it this way and that; gazing at it all the while with that impersonal and mild concentration peculiar to mother monkeys finding fleas on their young. He was curious, almost amused.

Then suddenly, horror seized him; and he started to bang and scramble crazily about the cage, dragging his dead side after him, yelling, hysteric.

Said Mi-Lang-Fu to his pupils in Tientsin: "Let X equal the unknown quantity. When X is found, life will cease. Because X is, and will be, unbearable."

Fifty pages of this, and then nothing. Who read it? No one, I remember—perhaps mistakenly. Yet I think there lived in me, along with the male and female that formed this spiritual hermaphrodite, another disturbing pair: creator and critic. C-1 would make something, C-2 would doubt it, or kill it. C-1 was full of illusions that C-2 would dissipate. Or was it the man who said "I am good." and the woman who said, "Never good enough, because I am a woman?"

All this inside a façade so assured, it seemed, so buoyant and certain that only the few who knew me best saw the ghost of fifteen praying to be beautiful and loved.

Apparently one man, forgotten now, though I seemed to have held him dear, did not. For during this period I wrote him a sonnet which began: "And so you have no faith; and want to cry 'Whore!/Teaser, deceiver, trivial-bodied child!'" and ended "If I adore/The interchange of hands, of words, of eyes/With this and that one, why should you ingrow/With bitterness, and bitterly despise/This playful heart, when any fool would know/In whose slim breast so much of it still lies!"

This was not, admittedly, much comfort for him. Nor do

I doubt that during the same week, an entry like this one appeared in my journal of that year: '31.

It is conceivable that disease will be split and resolved into two main categories: expressive and repressive. The expressive diseases are those which cause outward and visible deterioration or disturbance of the human body, and in so doing, dissipate their power. The repressive diseases are those which work inwardly—toward the core instead of away from it—and, having no outlet, increase constantly in strength. The expressive diseases are disappearing from the earth gradually; the repressive ones—such as cancer and cardiac complications—are gaining hold.

In cancer we seem to be dealing with *inverted* life; that is, creative force turned against itself. A sort of inward and destructive birth. I have often thought that this might be a vengeance of nature against a human's failure to create life outside himself—either emotional or physical. This creative power, then, with which every human is endowed to lesser or greater degree, finding insufficient outlet, turns inside him and destroys him. The living cell will not be frustrated.

By 1933 it had become evident that I could not go on living as I was and paying rent without getting a steady job. At the same time, too, the small apartment adjoining the family one, but self-contained, was now free. And although it seemed a retreat, almost abject, to be once more within the fold—even with walls between and a separate entrance—I had no choice.

So, armed with references from literary friends who

thought I could write, I started to make the rounds of newspapers and magazines.

After two failures, I found myself in the elegant offices of *Vogue,* with a note to Mrs. Edna Woolman Chase, its Editor-in-Chief. I had already sent ahead a few samples of prose, on request, and was ushered into her office, pastel and dainty and full of fresh white flowers.

She, too, was dainty and pastel, a small woman with alert appealing features framed by soft gray hair, all exquisitely groomed. I—in marked and lamentable contrast—was the bull in the china shop. Huge, with a sort of tousled bob and bangs, a turtleneck sweater, and a skirt that dragged at the hems.

Looking at me with a smile but ill-concealed pain, she asked me to sit. After talking about what *Vogue* wanted and what I thought I might be able to do, she said:

"My dear, I can see you have a very good pen"—and she rustled lightly the pages I sent her on the desk—"and I'm sure that in time—when you have been with us here for a while—we can help you develop a sense of style!" Her eyes here traveled over my rumpled self.

She took me on as copy-writer at $55.00 a week; I thanked her profusely and went home in triumph. Fifty-five dollars a *week!*

For a while my earth-shattering talents were used to write captions for spreads featuring things like corsets and handbags, or little paragraphs about accessories.

Though accepted without demur, it became increasingly clear that fashion was not my forte, either worn or described; so little by little I found myself producing items on theater or exhibitions of art until within a matter of months I became assistant to the feature editor, and later that editor myself.

My counterpart on *Vanity Fair,* next door on the nineteenth floor of the Graybar building, was Clare Booth Brokaw (later Luce), beautiful and brilliant and definitely daunting. That I felt I was no match for her, that we lived on different wave lengths, and that my job was to slowly absorb in *Vogue* the features of the dying *Vanity Fair:* these were not conducive to sisterhood. She was polite and helpful, but the less I had to tangle with her, the freer I breathed. She was the kind of woman who makes all other women want to give up.

Until, that is, I debated with her in Washington twenty-seven years later, in 1960, before the Newspaper Editors of America, substituting for an indisposed Eleanor Roosevelt. I was torn between enormous pride that Mrs. Roosevelt had suggested me, and an equal dread of what Mrs. Luce might do to me.

She had already called *The Reporter* to tell its promotion editor two things: first that Miss Mannes was not to consider this in the nature of a personal debate, and second that she wished to speak first.

The first request seemed to imply that I was no lady, the second struck me as a tactical error strangely unlike her.

But so far the worst of this was that I had only a week to prepare a script on our common topic (twenty minutes on What Is Wrong with Our Press?) and that I had to make a speech at Dartmouth in the middle of it.

Somehow, of course, I got to Washington, arriving at the Statler Hotel for the preceding dinner given by the Women's National Press Club dressed in what I had hoped was my best (a simple black chiffon) and clutching a sheaf of messy pages in my trembling hands.

Mrs. Luce was calm and inordinately beautiful; diamond-hung. The head table was full of awesome celebrities, including Turner Catledge, then managing editor of the New York *Times*, and Henry Luce.

One look at the audience gave me the shakes. During dinner I could recognize only too clearly the mixture of senators, Supreme Court judges, high-ranking diplomats, heads of government departments, and Washington correspondents scattered among the newspaper editors of the country.

The long preceding agony of food I could not eat and small talk I could not make and introductions essential to these ceremonies did not help. Neither did a swift comparison, when Mrs. Luce rose to make her address, between the impeccably typed and spiral-bound pages on the lectern before her and my collection of multi-corrected and scotch-taped pages and insertions.

Then the miracle happened. Mrs. Luce gave a precise but rather dull speech which elicited what they call polite—and certainly not long—applause.

I drew a deep breath when I got to the lectern and let go. What happened then I still find hard to believe. At the end, there was a standing ovation. During it, bowing and stunned, I looked briefly at Mrs. Luce and for the first time was sad for her.

Yet my speech angered her sufficiently to bring her back to the lectern in sharp rebuttal, and an unscheduled debate between us then took place. "There was blood," said Scotty Reston, "all over the place."

But for once, not mine. It might be revealing to add, however, that although the speech had wide repercussions in Washington and all over the country, only the woman's page of the Washington *Post* featured it prominently, no other newspaper printed it in full or in substantial part, and *Time* omitted it entirely.

• • •

Those three years at Condé Nast had, in any case, launched me into a world I had never known before. The world of the taste-makers, the fashion powers, the decorators of women and life; the beautiful, the talented, the homosexual; the rich, the titled, the conspicuous. Exquisites of society, here and abroad.

I was at once fascinated and scornful, amused and rebellious. Inside the works, so to speak, yet outside the world they moved and were moved by. The same day I would be photographed by Cecil Beaton (doubling sometimes as model) in diamonds and ermine, I would be striding the New York streets in tweeds and loafers (or their equivalent).

The night after a dazzling party among the Right People at Condé Nast's (the With-It people of then) I would be huddling with the Roosevelt-lovers they hated.

For, ironically, the year 1933 was to mark my late political awakening, not only through the emergence of the two great poles, Roosevelt and Hitler, but in rebellion against the glossy trivialities of the wealthy society now exposed to my view.

By nature elitist—in that I believed then as I do now in an aristocracy of mind and spirit—I rejected even more forcibly the artificial elites of wealth, family, fashion, and public relations. Faced with the pampered Beautiful, page after page, with languid nobility and their languorous parties, my heart more and more encompassed the "ugly" musicians, the out-of-work actors, the intense young artists and innovators, the indignant voices of the New Deal, and the rising American conscience.

Like all young women with a zest for life, I vastly enjoyed

some facets of my new *Vogue* existence, especially now that I wrote a theater column as well as edited and often initiated the magazine's other features. I felt both great admiration and affection for Mrs. Chase, respect and liking for many of my colleagues. Through my job I met some of the most talented artists, photographers, and designers of that era, had access to places and occasions not otherwise seen.

And then, wonderful weeks of vacation in England, or France, or Bermuda: passages of idle loving, privileges of position. Wherever an editor of *Vogue* might be, the glamour implicit in her title was bequeathed to her person. Those contemptuous of such assets have not had them.

Yet I had become increasingly worried about what might happen to me if I continued at *Vogue*. I saw other editors who had been there much longer than I make their jobs their life, their source of all life. If they were married, their obsession with the magazine was the paramount tie. If they weren't, they might never be: what man could offer this abundance, this continuous festival?

I saw myself gradually becoming like them, and it frightened me. I was frightened of something else too. There had been too many mornings of self-rebuke: the smell of drink, the mouth all blurred with kissing, the rumpled sheets stale with smoke, the taste of waste.

(Why did I do this, without real intention? Did I truly want this man (or that), or just want to be wanted? Had it become a reflex of submission, to prove that I could submit, that I was—just a woman? Did I make love because the one I loved had gone and I needed closeness, even with little desire? Was I investing a purely physical need with higher dimensions? What would happen to me if this went on and on, without some end in sight: some total love? Some resolution?)

Whatever was wrong, something had to be changed. I had to leave *Vogue*. After three years, two raises, and even strong hints from both Condé Nast and Mrs. Chase that I might inherit her job, I knew I could not go on. Not from nine to five every day, month after month; year after year.

(What was your fourth ghost doing, Wohleben asks, going on thirty and still unformed, unresolved? Were you thinking that marriage and children were part of life, and that in your gluttony for living you had to have this too? Were you slowly succumbing to the need for security you disdained in other women: the protective shelter of one man you could love?)

Maybe. But I thought of the shelter too, which would give me the chance to write what I wanted to write. No time for this any more, no distance for thought, even though I had managed in my spare time to write a long narrative poem about the city I loved and hated: mine.

Or, more particularly, about five New Yorkers drinking and spilling their guts out to each other in a speak-easy. It was called *Hexad,* and this was the tenor of it:

The Jew bent forward in his chair
And pinioned everybody there
With urgent glances, lowering
His voice for closer listening.

"Nor evolution, nor chemistry, nor stars, nor suns,
Nor laws of gravity, nor equations and axioms,
Nor all the wisdom of scientists and philosophers,
Historians and biologists and masons
Brought into being this city. Only one thing,
One force could ever conceive
Child as horrendous and irrational,
As splendid and tragic and unnatural as New York.

One thing, one force, one will—and that a stupendous
Splendid, cruel, unreasoning god—
Jehovah!
Jeohovah! Yahveh! Hysterical molder of beauty
Built for his own destroying of it, and so
All the stronger for its mortality.
Jehovah, the Lord, God, Jupiter, Ammon—any divinity
is only
Human genius, with its attendant corruptions, stretched
to enormity.
For this I worship God, as I worship myself for
bringing forth a fugue—
For this alone, allowing his corruptions,
Must any God be worshiped. Amen," said Aaron.

• • •

"Ignore 'em. I was speaking of angels," said Aaron,
"and what they were hearing."
Then Oppenheim rose up, with darkling brown
Sinus contorted, fiercer than Radnick's, held out his
arms,
Gnarled and black-haired, and bellowed:
"Is there no one among you to exalt New York?
Is there no one?
No one to understand the city
Beyond her angles and her complexity,
Beyond her immensity?
Is there no one?
So cries Jehovah, despairing.
From his too-weary brain the city tore itself,
Leaving a monstrous wound that yearns for healing,
will not heal
Without revelation!
But there was only the answering of wings
Whirring and beating, and no archangels

Or angels spoke, until
Smoke-swaddled, Gabriel came to the Lord and said
these things,
A trifle acidulous:
'Lord, call not upon the observers for revelation,
But on the doers;
Ask not of ministers the meaning of love,
But of wooers.
We are the critics, Lord, never the makers,
We are the takers, Lord, never the givers.
Only the atom lost in the city knows the city.
Angels can only watch, can only pity.
Call not upon the observers, Lord, for revelation.'
Said Gabriel."

. . .

They turned to Arnold.
Turned to his ivory delicate face
Made little by the constant trace
Of irony; to his fine nose
Made thin and precious by a pose
Of weary silent sufferance;
And to the melancholy glance
Of pale and heavy-lidded eyes
Determined to deny surprise;
And to his slight-portioned chin,
To lips that no amount of gin
Could broaden and make warm. At these
Reflections of the man they stared,
Wanting him to begin,
Prepared—.

"New York is an avalanche, in acceleration.
New York is an avalanche of girders and stone,
Of crowds and ideas, bodies and bricks and books,
And people—innumerable but alone.

New York is a cataract of fancy and fact
Doomed to a union of mutual desecration—
Debussy and jazz played at one time, together,
Inevitably, surely killing each other."

Uneven and sprawling as this was, over fifty-one pages, it aroused the interest of editors and writing friends, and in one instance serious thought of publication.

But again I was told it was not "suitable": too off-beat, too out of key with what magazines wanted. Too long for them, too short for a book, and so on.

I accepted the verdict meekly enough. But at the same time the thought nagged at my mind (as it still does now): surely things no better than this and even worse are published now. Why these rejections?

With this history of failure as a free-lance, how could I live after I left the security of *Vogue?* How could I possibly afford to experiment till I hit my stride—whatever on earth that might be?

• • •

In these same years the rest of my family had certainly hit *their* stride. My mother and father, known for a long time now for their deeply sensitive command of sonata music, both in concerts abroad and here, had by now given up their public performances to be full-time co-directors of the Mannes Music School (now Mannes College of Music) they started in 1916. They both believed deeply that the training of musicians was not merely a matter of mastering an instrument but of developing human creativity as a whole, of enlarging mind and spirit. To achieve this meant not only the best faculty available but a close individual relationship between teacher and student and between student and the directors themselves. My father was a constant presence in his school, his charm and gentleness pervading the place. As usual, he talked to children as he did to others: father-confessor to the child as he was, inevitably, romantic image to women. This would have worried my mother even more than it did (she joked about it although it hurt her in the one area of confidence she lacked) if my father were not inherently a domestic man, deeply committed to her and us. In all his years as violinist, concertmaster, conductor, and teacher, he had met many women of fame and beauty, among them Ethel Barrymore and Isadora Duncan, whom he worshiped; and such women inevitably gravitated toward him.

But the woman he married was part of him, and he wrote this of her in 1937:

> Clara was to find the fulfillment of her musical life, of her great talents and capacities of mind and heart, in directing the growing school. Without her, this important crux of our lives would have been impossible. It needed her loyal adherence to the highest standards of art and spirit of music, and her clear judgment in the consideration of necessary details, to give unified expression to our combined vision. Alone neither of us could accomplish our destined work. What I lack in clarity and courage and decisiveness she provided. And I, perhaps, contribute a certain philosophy and a certain phantasy—which sometimes appears to be irrational if not downright mad—without which no vision can be sustained.

During this same decade, the color-process which my brother, Leopold, and Leo Godowsky had spent nine years perfecting at Eastman's in Rochester, was in production. Kodachrome came on the market in the spring of 1935. The joint spark first ignited in the minds of two seventeen-year-old schoolboys, both musicians, had hit business and the press as a happy phenomenon and a major Kodak achievement.

But music won again. Over the next decades, Leopold turned over the greater part of his Kodachrome royalties to support his parents' school, returned to the piano, and formed a trio in which he and the late Luigi Silva and Bronislaw Gimpel played both across the continent and in Europe. He was also involved peripherally in a score of other musical activities, happiest always in the familiar mix of science and sound. Although he had majored in physics at Harvard, where he was asked to stay on as instructor, his restless and all-encompassing mind had that leap of association between diverse disciplines which is a large element of genius, and which demanded dual expression as inventor and musician. Not only were these capacities extraordinarily developed in him, but accompanied—as all who knew him would testify—by charm and wit and extraordinary kindness.

Although my father and brother were very different people, I have often wondered whether as the dominating male images of my youth they had not made it hard for me to love lesser men. They were a tough act to follow.

And even though I now had a full external life of my own, I shared this heady mix whenever I could. Between absences, long or short, my family was a source of recurrent stimulation, support, and mutual love.

And although I was still a little scared of my mother, I could—as always—speak with my father about everything. He never judged.

• • •

No diary recorded these events and my own pulls and drives, but in the winter of '35 and '36 I began to see more and more of a handsome, complex, and talented American with the means to live partly in Florence and partly in this country as a serious painter. Though he was never satisfied with what he did and often let his canvases unfinished, his painting struck me as haunting and lyrical: the product of a poetic and immensely cultivated perception.

In the spring of 1936 I left *Vogue* and went to live with him in Florence. His home was the most beautiful place I had ever seen: a Medicean villa on top of a hill beyond the city and across the river from Fiesoli. Miles of Tuscan terraced hills like this one spread out below and beyond to the clear horizons of Giorgione or Piero della Francesca. The ancient folds of this marvelous land were velvet shadows.

The owner of this domain, my host, had made every part of the villa and its gardens a visual feast, inside and out. It was a fusion of love and knowledge and perfectionism that I had never known, and thanks to him, a continuing education of the eye.

To live on this hill of beauty and luxury isolated from the ever tightening vise of Fascism was an anomaly fully recognized by us both. Below in Florence and in all the Italian towns we visited, the childish and pompous slogans of the Duce strutted in black letters across yellow or ocher or orange walls. On public radios his voice exhorted his people to the glorious prides and wars of idiots. And on the shortwave radio in the villa, the far more terrible screeches of Hitler scratched the air and clawed at the fearful mind.

Although the omens of a monstrous collision course were brutally clear, they were blurred by the rationalization of most human beings evading reality. These dictators, these maniacs, can't get away with it. It is bluff and bluster, however hideous. And besides, what can one do? Would we blunt the edge of dictatorship, help tip the axis of tyranny, if we left Italy, abandoned this home?

Perhaps people of greater conscience would have done just that. Instead, in the winter months in New York in '37 we married and then returned to the villa for two more years.

But I did very little writing there. This was a world of the senses and it drew me back powerfully to the sculpture I thought abandoned. I was given the lemon house under the villa—a stone arcade facing the Tuscan hills—as studio. Materials of every kind were close at hand; so also the marvelous Italian craftsmen; almost always there to work on the continuing additions to the villa's grounds: terraces, grottos, fountains designed by its never-satisfied owner, then redesigned.

So while he painted and supervised the household at large (the staff of servants had been with him through a former marriage and needed no coaching) I worked in the lemon house, on heads and figures and bas-reliefs until—to my great joy—I was permitted to make a Madonna to replace her crumbled remnant in the roadside shrine near the villa. There was just enough of her left to indicate her position and the fall of her robes; and the angel of the annunciation kneeling before her dictated the style of the period in form and color. I was deeply touched and proud when the villagers accepted the new Madonna and blessed the shrine.

This fundamental religiosity impelled me also to make a huge bas-relief of the head and arms of Christ on the cross, a strange work later embedded in a wall of the villa. It is the face of a tortured man, now finally at peace.

In a turnabout, I also made a torso of a voluptuous and bacchanalian nymph who may still be laughing above a grotto fountain, for all I know.

In between these various efforts and preoccupations, I drove through much of Italy with the most knowledgeable guide to its centuries of creative splendor that I could have had.

Yet at the villa a sense of isolation, of loneliness slowly grew. The *gente per bene*—the old established society of Florence, of which many were friends of my husband, and especially of his former wife—now ostracized both of us because I had lived with him before marrying him. They had come in force to a party officially introducing me as his wife, were utterly charming, and never seen again. I was not once asked to their homes, and wholly boycotted at concerts or public occasions. We had only a very few close friends—a liberal lawyer and his wife, a musician and his wife, occasional visitors (largely non-Florentine) to talk to. I did not brood on this—there was too much else to enjoy—but for a gregarious American it was strange, incredible.

That summer of 1938 Hitler and Mussolini met in Florence. On the day this was to happen most prudent citizens stayed home and all known dissidents were cleared from sensitive areas.

I walked alone down the long hill to Florence, impelled to see what I hated and dreaded most.

The route of the dictators' passage was not made public. The streets were therefore unusually empty for that mecca of tourists and, in fact, for any Italian city. Little clumps of people stood at several intersections and along the Arno, but their silence was strange and unusual. As I wandered around the streets I heard only one noise, repeated at intervals. It came from loudspeakers attached to the cornices of buildings. From a crackling, highly amplified sound track they roared

"Duce! Duce! Duce!" as from the mouths of watching masses.

After almost an hour of this, bored, I retraced my steps to the Ponte di Ferro, and finding an air of expectancy in the group clustered there by the river, decided to join them.

In no more than ten minutes, with no warning, they drove along the Lungarno toward us in an open car: Hitler and Mussolini side by side. As they turned slowly toward the Ponte di Ferro they were no more than twelve feet away. In that frozen minute I noticed two things. Hitler's mustache and hair were rusty, not black as the pictures showed them. And, next to him, Mussolini looked like a human being. Several people raised their arms and cried "Duce! Duce!", but the rest seemed dazed.

I was, myself. All I could think of all the way up the hill to Piazza Calda was that I could have thrown some flowers and a bomb with ease into that car. And that I would have happily died for having done so.

• • •

It was in this beauty and isolation that I wanted a child. My husband had already a son of eight who lived with us from time to time, and I doubt if his urge for another being was as strong as mine.

But the pregnancy was a time of total happiness and peace; and for once I questioned nothing. It taught me at least what other women told me they felt: a sense of completion and worth, a "reason for being." I had never believed this, and I do not now. It can be, and has been for millennia, the sanctioned goal of a woman's life: what more need she do, or be?

So then I did nothing but grow immense and proud.

We returned to New York in the sixth or seventh month so

that the child would be born an American citizen. The birth was long and not easy, even with drugs, but when they brought me this nine and a half pounds of boy I couldn't believe it.

There—really there—a child. And I was a mother.

• • •

In love, yes, but not in nurture. A nurse was already waiting at home. There would always be nurses. What did I know about taking care of a child, free soul over thirty, always in other worlds? No more prepared to be a mother than his sire a father?

But then I saw nothing wrong in nurses if they were good and one could afford them. The guilt came much later, a decade later, when mothers as non-instinctive as myself were told of their crime. The crime of deprivation: to deprive an infant of the continuous closeness of his mother. A deprivation during the first five years of life, they were told, that would mar, or scar, or diminish a child for life.

We know it now, more than ever in this alienated and hostile society, where the only real communication lies in these primal acts of love and touch; man and woman, mother and child, father and child, human and human. What else endures?

But once maternal demands began to impinge, I began to retreat. Like most men who have successfully dodged for millennia the actual nurture of child and home (owed equally with their women) I wanted to pull free from the basic hourly, daily matters of care. I loved to hold my child but not diaper him. To play with him but not always to bathe him. The only routine I really loved was breast feeding: sensual, miraculously complete. But factors beyond my will curtailed even this.

The curse of the romantic is a greed for dreams, an intensity of expectation that, in the end, diminishes the reality. I had thought of marriage as a complete sharing, of family as a trinity in which mother and father would together raise, instruct, and delight in the child. Had I not been that child? Another woman faced with another reality might, in reaction, have become more fiercely maternal. Out of fear—the fear of a palpable male jealousy—I did not. It was a cowardice that has never stopped haunting me; an evasion of clear responsibility for which I find no excuse.

The photographs then show a radiant mother with a beautiful child. What more could a woman want that she did not have? The answer, however true, was no absolution.

• • •

Even before that, we knew we had to leave. War was imminent, the thought of being trapped in Italy, impotent, with our child, was unthinkable. Each of us felt that somehow, someway we would have to involve ourselves in the coming battle.

As a final punctuation, the *Questura* (Florentine police) had come to the villa to check on me. The *signore's* wife was partly Jewish, was she not? Then the *signore* could anticipate certain—embarrassments, shall we say?—as a result of enforcing the new laws on person of Jewish blood. The *signore* did. Everybody was very polite.

• • •

In August of '39 we packed our belongings and left the villa and the people we loved, among them—and foremost—the wonderful man who took care of it and us. We left with sadness and deep forebodings.

In Paris, briefly, my husband confirmed his decision to stay in France and find out what he, as an American, could do to work for the Allies, in any capacity. I was to go back with the baby and nurse and await developments in New York.

On board the *Aquitania,* September 2, two days out from New York the news of war came through. The brilliant terraces of light on the big Cunarder were blacked out at night, and the talk was of submarines and horror as we ate and drank.

The baby flourished in infant oblivion; a dispeller of shadows and a signal of hope.

• • •

In the next two years we led a normal New York life, underlaid, however, by a state of suspension. My husband had returned not long after, and alternated his usual painting days in his studio with regular hours at Roosevelt Field learning to fly small planes.

I spent at least half a day at another small studio near home involved in a growing absorption in portrait heads. The faces of people had always fascinated me. Years before my brother, Leopold, and I had pored over books on genetics and phrenology, increasingly sure that there were distinct and repeated patterns in bone and tissue which gave clues to character. We had observed, however erroneously in the light of present knowledge, that in people of superior intelligence the space from the top of the ear to the top of the skull was higher than average, and the frontal lobes over the brows markedly thicker. We were sure that triangular nostrils on women indicated a chronic emotionalism not unlike hysteria; that men with convex features were more aggressive than the concave ones. And so on.

We wondered why women with buck teeth and receding chins were inclined to be amiable and funny, and whether large noses on men were indeed matched with large cocks, and why.

Now I had in my possession a remarkable book published in Germany called *Das Ewige Antlitz* ("The Eternal Countenance"). It consisted of death masks of great men, reaching as far back as Henry the Fourth of France and forward as far as Nietzsche. It was, and continues to be, a source of revelation as well as mystery.

The face of a poet is that of Napoleon. The face of a madman belongs to Swift. Wagner is beatific in death. Nietzsche tortured, St. Beuve at once ironical and benign.

Armed with this, a familiarity with anatomy, a stand, some armatures, tools, a bucket of clay, and a good north light, I went to work.

Most of my sitters were men. Not only because of my old generic love, but because their bones are more visible and defined. Also, I was lucky in knowing some remarkable men with remarkable faces.

For two years I worked very hard and very happily. Thanks to my husband, I could afford to indulge myself in the luxury of not having to earn: it was a labor of love.

It was also far more rewarding sensuously than writing. I could feel with my fingers not only the clay but the living features before me: the lips, the temples, the hair, the sockets of the eyes, the cranial mass.

I seemed to need very few sittings and very short ones. I had noticed how faces went dead at a certain point, and how the clarity of my own observation could blur. Also, most of my sitters had little time.

My own, for that matter, was spent more without them than with them. After the impetus of the actual presence, I could, without it and with greater freedom, give memory and insight fuller play.

Alone, also, I could turn on the radio to the music that I most loved; the universal design that animated all form.

I had not then any illusions about the importance of this work except to me; and I have not now. It was proficient, and some of the likenesses were fresh and true. But I knew already that it was an anachronism at a time when art was pulling further and further away from the external appearance of things to internal translation. Who now, in any event, wanted a bust in the house, or the modern flat? A college president, perhaps, a chairman of a board, or some general. But it was not their faces I wanted to feel and recreate. Not for any niche in a pantheon, for any money.

Knowing this, I knew also that it was an escape and a self-indulgence at a time when only a person of genius could rationalize either. The daily news pounded at me, lacerated. Isolation from the life or death of peoples and civilization itself was unpardonable. To remain passive in the face of this giant evil, to use family, sex, or talent as reason for withdrawal: How could I, and face myself? I had to get into the arena and fight, with whatever weapons I had, and if only with words.

By that time my husband was already about to enter the Naval Air Force, having obtained his pilot's license; and many friends, even before '42, were applying for jobs in any sector of the Allied effort they could qualify for.

So when I was asked to join a small unofficial group in the winter of '40–'41 concerned with co-ordinating information from occupied countries, I accepted. My languages would presumably be of help, they said, and my knowledge of Europeans and their conditions.

• • •

The marriage had by that time turned an ugly corner into destruction, acerbated by war.

For some men, war is a tragedy. For many more, in those years, war was a release. Not only a release from passivity into action, or from routine into raw engagement. It was a release also from responsibilities unsought or now grown irksome, and from human confrontations somehow to be evaded. I know, because two years later I could excuse the same release and evasion on the same honorable grounds: to fight for country. (The man in the woman understands the man.)

By the time we entered World War II, the flyer had flown. It was much easier to make specific and urgent requests for divorce from a distant port than face emotional scenes at home (there had been enough, God knows); and nothing you had to explain to a four-year-old.

• • •

5.

The group I had joined was called the International Coordination Council, or ICC. It consisted of several distinguished prewar refugees, now U.S. citizens, and Americans who hoped to channel their knowledge and talents into constructive use against the Axis enemies. They had, above all, valuable links to the European underground, chiefly within labor, business, and intellectual circles. One of the group's self-imposed jobs was to maintain these contacts wherever possible and by whatever means, to read all clandestine reports, to learn what we could from the few who managed, often in great danger, to leave their beleaguered homes, and to correlate all this for transmittal to the appropriate government departments.

Because I happened to be one of the few then interested in mass communications—in radio, since television's power was not yet unleashed—my suggestion that I learn what I could from the foreign-language stations in New York became my function. I began to listen to the German and Italian broadcasts that still—after Pearl Harbor—spoke to the minority groups of this tri-state region.

What I heard made me suspicious and at times incredulous. Enough, in fact, to enlist—with the council's approval—two stringers to listen at regular intervals and submit reports. They were also to report the identities and backgrounds of the broadcasters.

Many, it soon appeared, had long histories of pro-Nazi and pro-Fascist sympathies and affiliations, and although most were clever in muting them, they were equally clever on air conveying a surface neutrality which could fool the unalert ear. They could not, however, fool a reporter on the weekly *Aufbau,* who wrote as follows on December 12, 1941:

> . . . And the first German language broadcast of the New York Radio Station WBNX began, after the American declaration of war on Japan on Monday, 8:15 P.M., even before the German announcer started talking, with *Auf in den Kampf Torero* . . . —although German broadcasts as a rule only offer German music! To comment on the first day of war, which, on account of the sudden, cowardly attack of the Japanese, was not a lucky one for America, they played *Ach du lieber Augustin* and this, as was emphasized by the announcer "upon request" . . . Even before this, the two German announcers of WBNX used to give musical comments to the military situation, which were incomprehensible for American observers who were not familiar with the words and the contents of the song. Thus the German broad-

cast brought the Victory March from *Aida* two weeks ago, when the British were thrown back in Libya . . . And on Armistice Day, when President Roosevelt had spoken, the well-known Irish folk song *The Rosary* was played—but with the translated, overemphasized title *Der Rosenkranz* . . .

Reports like this, furthermore kept coming in.

These men can choose any records they want and play them in any order at any time on their broadcasts. Very often they play request numbers; that is, individuals call up the station requesting certain pieces and the producer of that particular program complies at his convenience. There is no check on the persons requesting the program. For the most part they are merely voices over the telephone. There is, therefore, no control and no supervision. The program managers may choose the records ten minutes before they go on the air. They need account to no one for their choice. It takes no hysterical imagination to see the potential danger in this.

These and a growing mass of disquieting evidence impelled the council to set up a separate committee not only for this kind of monitoring but as a possible screening agency for foreign personnel of proven allegiance to the Allied cause who could be useful not only for foreign-language broadcasting here but more especially to the Office of War Information, whose offices were then in New York and which was not then by law permitted to employ aliens.

The original committee consisted of two others, a man and

woman of outstanding political intelligence and valuable contacts, and myself. While they were establishing the connections with the OWI, which subsequently turned us into a formal entity called Short Wave Research under subcontract to that operation, I had decided on my own to bring the results of this local monitoring of foreign language broadcasts to the attention of the Federal Communications Commission in Washington. I knew no one there, but in the inconceivable event that they did not know what was going over these stations across the country, I thought I would send a report—merely as a concerned American—of our findings. In my long letter I suggested particularly that they examine the business of "request" musical numbers. This seemed an ideal setup for coded messages to agents and even to the submarines doubtless cruising within range.

The letter caused sufficient interest for a meeting with a member of the FCC and an expression of thanks. They did not have the staff, he said, to monitor these small stations with any regularity, but they would look into the matter further.

There seemed no particular urgency in his manner, but I had done what I could and left it at that: bemused.

My second worry concerned the astrology columns in the *Staats-Zeitung,* an entirely respectable and established German paper in New York. This was triggered by a report from a faithful source asked to keep an eye on the local foreign press:

You know that I am convinced that the Nazis here, American citizens or not, are making every effort to keep their lines of communication open. And I have told you that, knowing a bit about Nazi mentality and Nazi technique, I am convinced they are doing it via the *Staats-Zeitung*. Thus, when I happened to read the "horoscope" I really must say I got the surprise of my life.

Here are the essential excerpts of the last three horoscopes in translation. Please read them as if you were a Nazi, and looking at them for guidance:

December 9th:

". . . Meet unforeseen situations with calm and diplomacy, do not travel today and pay attention to your nerves . . . Unexpected successes should be expected during the 12 months to come, the favorable consequences of which are possible, however, only if the people born under today's star (*Sternzeichenkinder*) are restricting themselves intuitively (*Gefuehlsmaessig*) and if they are checking their business relations carefully with regard to this./And tomorrow? Do not risk anything extraordinary. Go into details./How to meet the next danger days? December 17th: Content yourself also with step by step successes; December 23rd: No unconsidered decisions . . .

"And tomorrow? Do not let the heart decide over your thoughts; intuitive excitements can easily destroy your well-constructed plans./What has the new year of life in store? December 17th: Be content also with partial successes; December 23rd: Do not mislead yourself during the evening to unconsidered decisions."

This advice (wrote the monitor) is coming from far. By short wave??? Again the old advice is not to let their attention be distracted by secondary matters and not to turn up too much in public.

I realize that it will be difficult to find out what really is behind these writings, but considering the fact that the Nazis, prior to 1933, have used exactly the same way of instructing their followers by harmless-looking newspaper items, I think it worthwhile to draw your special attention to this.

I am more than ever convinced that the Nazis purposely are keeping quiet their sabotage groups here for the time being, and that they are intending to give the signal to them only after a special and great occasion will make their activity more useful to them.

I am entirely at your disposal in connection with these things, and I am continuing to read the *Staats-Zeitung,* though—as you will realize—I always have to go home for reading it since it is not advisable for a refugee now to read a German-language paper in public.

My third unease concerned the sudden, very marked rise in the sale of diathermy sets, especially along the New Jersey, Long Island, and northeast coast beyond. The sets were widely advertised over German-language stations as a great alleviator of rheumatism and arthritis. They could also, I learned, be easily and quickly converted into short wave radios by anyone handy with electronic parts.

Again, the submarines. What better way to transmit requested data?

By the time I had passed these various musings along to persons in a position to corroborate them or dismiss them, I had already moved with my colleagues into a midtown office with the letters SHORT WAVE RESEARCH, INC. printed on the glass door, and myself on the letterhead as President. I felt this was silly considering our vestigial size and function, but there had, it seemed, to be such an officer. My new married name, moreover, was incontrovertibly American to offset the "foreign" given one.

For about two years, our major job bore little relation to our title. It consisted largely of interviewing hundreds of refugees from France and Italy and Germany and Austria and Czechoslovakia as a preliminary to possible use in the Office of War Information. Those who were recommended by us were then sent on to the OWI. If they were accepted by the agency as broadcast writers or speakers or researchers, they were technically employed and paid for by us.

I interviewed chiefly the German-speaking contingent, my partner the Latins. It was often interesting, always enlightening, and too often deeply sad.

In the case of those we found suspicious (our antennae grew progressively longer as the job went on), I sent their dossiers along to the Office of Strategic Services, the OSS, with our reservations. We also sent dossiers on those we felt might be more useful to intelligence operations than to the OWI.

In the winter of 1943 I was approached by the OSS for a possible job. The standard protracted process of screening by the FBI had apparently turned up nothing to question my patriotic, if not my personal, purity.

But something else had. A southern congressman had formed a committee to investigate what he termed—in effect if not in official terms—"interference with the constitutional freedom of the air waves." This presumably described certain investigations of foreign-language radio programs and personnel in the New York area. Somewhere, inevitably, my name popped up as one of the iniquitous interferers. The records of Short Wave Research, Inc. were subpoenaed, and I found myself shortly—and with dismay—involved in a series of star-chamber hearings later climaxed by a full Committee hearing in Washington. Since what little I had done had been, I thought, the patriotic duty of an American citizen, this was an ugly shock.

It gradually transpired, of course, that they were not out to get me, but to find in Short Wave Research and its sub-rosa, subcontract relationship with the government Office of War Information a handy club to beat President Roosevelt with. Those people running the OWI—like Robert Sherwood and Elmer Davis—fuzzy do-gooders and intellectuals and their New Deal ilk—were getting away with un-American, undercover stuff.

It was not only a deeply disturbing and even frightening experience for me, but would—I felt sure—effectively bar any direct government service. That it did not was due to the direct assurance by Sherwood to Allen Dulles of my integrity as a person and loyalty as a citizen. But for weeks it had left me shaking at every phone call, every envelope with a government imprint, however routine the contents turned out to be.

• • •

My first job at the OSS Counter-Intelligence section, then based in offices at Rockefeller Center, was to reorganize their files. I was to go through a large bank of cards pertaining to individuals, mostly foreign, and sort them out in the categories assigned.

God knows when these cards were first made and by whom. The two major categories were under the headings Friendly and Un-Friendly, and one that I shortly turned up was appallingly typical. I cannot remember, of course, the name and exact sector of the German High Command, but this will do:

"von Eberstadt-Ottlingen, Colonel Friederich Hans Albrecht, 47, . . . attached since 1937 to Ober Kommando Wehrmacht, etc. . . . Tall, blue-eyed, gray-blond hair. Has friendly smile . . ."

This was in the Friendly file.

It took three weeks and several secretaries to clear *that* mess up.

My next job there was called Intercepts, and for me sheer bliss. I could not only *read* other people's private letters but was *ordered* to, thus breaking a lifetime of discretion—in that area, at least. I had been briefed, of course, about the identity and ostensible business of the writers concerned. My job was by association and instinct to find out what, if anything, they were actually doing and through which connections. I doubt if my batting average was high, but a few things emerged.

In all such activities British agents assisted us. They were then—and continued to be wherever I found myself—of very great help.

In time I was sent to be groomed for other work. The grooming took place in a large sprawling apartment on the West Side. Here about six or eight of us, mostly men, were taught things that enthralled my Mata Hari soul. How to pick locks, how to piece together small bits of paper retrieved from trash, how to break codes, how to take photographs without being noticed, how to find things hidden in strange places. Since I was equally poor at picking locks and breaking codes, I marvel that I was not then kicked out of X2, as Counter-Intelligence was called.

They asked me instead to go to Portugal and Spain that summer. Since I had turned down a previous offer to go to their Washington headquarters and work there, I could hardly refuse this assignment. Nor could the Mata Hari syndrome be quelled. Since my motto in life has been "When in doubt, do," it seemed inevitable.

One part of me said that I should never leave a four-year-old child even with his adoring grandparents for a period of months at least. And in retrospect it is probably clear that I should not have done so.

But the man in me could not reject the easier challenge: flight, risk, the battle of wits, and above all a whack at the enemy. By then, after reading an endless stream of reports from the occupied countries and from Germany, after detailed exposure to the unparalleled horror of the concentration camps and Gestapo procedures, I was filled with a hatred of the Nazis so intense that anything I could do against them, however small, was an imperative act. The imperative act of being a mother was lost to a rationalization that no father ever has to make.

I had, of course, to acquire a cover. *The New Yorker* magazine, unable to base a correspondent in Lisbon through normal procedures, was pleased that with tacit government co-operation they could send me there. I was to write back regular "Letters" from Lisbon and Madrid, while paid by the OSS through unvouchered funds.

As for me, I had lately been seen in print often enough to have earned the credentials of writer and journalist.

So June third of 1944 found me on a clipper bound for Lisbon. It was my fortune that among the passengers was George Kennan, then finishing his term as U. S. Chargé d'Affaires in Portugal prior to leaving for a new post in Moscow. During the flight, delayed by a day in Bermuda, he told me more about the situation in Portugal than all I had learned from prior briefings.

Also on board was the director of an international business cartel based in Lisbon who was later to be of help in many ways, some of which he would not know.

We arrived at the mouth of the Tagus at dark in a shattering thunderstorm. It was the beginning of four months and a grade-B movie now too late to make. So many impressive spy stories have already been told that mine will get only the comedy treatment that it deserves.

B548 (or whatever my number was) was given no specific assignments beyond infiltration of suspected Fascist circles and an open ear.

She spent her time eavesdropping on any German handy and hanging around local dives with correspondents, friendly and otherwise.

She discovered in time that circles for infiltration, salons of nobility and upper class sympathetic to Germans, were presided over by hotesses not sympathetic to big blond American writers with pretensions to glamour. Discovered equally that the gentlemen were. So had no access to homes because Latin gentlemen preferred single dating outside. What is more, they refused to believe she was really a writer. ("What are you doing over here, a beautiful woman like you, alone?") Proof and protestations availing nothing, B548 changes her tack.

When asked what she does, she narrows her eyes and whispers: "Didn't you know, I am an international spy!" This breaks up the gents and the tension (partially). They think it is very funny, and only then open up. Spy then has to make concession, but just how far? Agent requests advice from local X2 superior, is told "As far as you need." Thanks a lot.

This dilemma prevails in Madrid too, only worse. Men more aggressive, stakes higher, risks increase. Ritz Hotel domicile a nest of Nazi agents who know perfectly well who big blonde is: the code used in X2 announcing my arrival was broken en route. Great help.

All very fascinating but very sticky. Reports as much as

she can elicit, walks on eggs. Is given her first Mickey Finn at home of industrialist making parachutes for the German, then seduced. Not pleasant at all. However, should have been warned. At earlier session in above man's office had been asked to pose on couch as Goya's Maja Desnuda. Demurred. Gentleman promises on his honor not to touch. B548 removes clothes, assumes pose, thinks of parachutes. Honor then kept, as per word.

Is then given instructions by superior (by messenger) for new pursuits. Memorize, tear up in tiny pieces, put into john and flush. They regurgitate twice. Mash them into a little ball and they go down. Why didn't they tell her that in New York?

By then had long since entertained conviction that as agent of counter-intelligence was total dud. Switched, without asking, to political intelligence, sent back copious reports about Spanish opposition to Axis as well as support: key figures, goals, and such.

Spent some hours hanging around airports in last month hoping to spot rats escaping from Germany to Latin countries via Spain and Portugal. Recognize German known fifteen years before in New York as beautiful bachelor and now as agent. Report at once.

• • •

And so on. I did my best but accomplished, I fear, very little. After the Allies had opened up France, in any case, it became the center of intelligence operations against the Nazis and the need for a concentration of agents in the Iberian Peninsula no longer existed. I returned to New York in September and wrote a long and lurid report to my OSS boss, which I fear molders somewhere but in which I at least refrained from requesting the Purple Heart for acts beyond the call of duty.

If my country derived any benefit from my services at all, aside from spicy reading, it was a lesson that henceforth no female as conspicuous as myself should be sent abroad as an agent, especially in Latin countries. And certainly not without a specific Code of Compliance.

As for my cover activities, they at least kept my countrymen informed as to the nature of nations ostensibly neutral but far from neutralized in a major war. The "Letters" from Madrid and Lisbon appeared as sent in *The New Yorker* that summer of 1944. My last journalist act in Lisbon was to send a requested article to *Vogue* on fashion in Lisbon. If nothing else, they show that three years in the world of clothes had not rubbed off.

• • •

The first thing I wrote after I was "demobilized" from the OSS in the spring of '45 was this account of the only enemy spy I grew to know well:

I met Paul Jean Marie Cavaillez in July 1944 in Madrid.

"Met" is possibly the wrong word: Cavaillez picked me up. I was lunching alone in the dining room of the Hotel Ritz in Madrid. Outside, the July heat was blinding on the streets, but inside the lofty white stately dining room a green reflected light from the garden filtered through the shaded windows, and a light breeze blew. Tail-coated waiters glided between the tables and wheeled along trays loaded with hors-d'oeuvres.

Alone at a table against the wall was a small old man who looked like a plucked bird: his narrow head was practically hairless, his nose was a beak, his hooded lids grayish pink. This was General Moscardo, hero of the siege of the

Alcázar—hero, that is, to Franco's army. Next to him, also eating alone, was a youngish man with round shoulders, graying hair and a thin face that did not look at all Spanish. We faced each other across the room. I noticed that he kept watching me. This was not in itself unusual, as in Spain unaccompanied women are rare enough to rivet male attention. They can, in fact, be only one of three things: prostitutes, agents, or crazy foreigners. As a member of the latter category, I kept my eyes on my plate or practiced that intricate art of timing wherein the observed examines the observer at those moments when the observer is not observing.

After paying forty-five pesetas (then about four dollars on the official exchange) for my six-course lunch (called the "little menu," as opposed to the "big menu" of eight courses), I went up to my room for the siesta without which a Spanish summer is unbearable. I was just dozing off when there was a knock at my door and a white-spatted bellboy about four feet high handed me a letter on a silver platter. He said an answer was expected, so I asked him to wait outside. The note was in French and was signed "Paul Cavaillez." "I noticed you in the dining room," it said, "and I would be enchanted [*ravi* was the word] to meet you later in the afternoon and have a little chat." It included a brief phrase which fascinated me with its lordliness: *"Vous me plaisez"*—"You please me." It was this phrase which stimulated my curiosity to the point of writing an affirmative note, saying I would meet him in the lobby at five o'clock. I gave the note back to the bellboy and went to sleep.

The meeting that afternoon was the first of a series of meetings with Paul Cavaillez that extended through my stay in Spain and were resumed in New York the following winter. I kept him waiting in the lobby of the Ritz that first time for half an hour. When we shook hands I noticed two things about him which remained, in my eyes at least, two of his three dominant features: his limp, moist hands and his extremely pale, wide-open eyes, like those of some night bird. The third was the stoop of his shoulders which made his head jut forward, not aggressively, but in a sort of chronic obsequiousness. His face, however, was as intelligent as his conversation proved to be later. He spoke an educated French in a voice which had no depth or substance—it was light and thin, and his laugh was in the same key.

In the course of our conversations, over drinks or meals, we talked of many things, among them life in Spain. Cavaillez was very derogatory about the Spaniards—their laziness, their corruption, their hypocrisy. In so far as he spoke of those now controlling Spain, I agreed with him. He had obviously no contact with the Spanish people. He seemed, in fact, to have little contact with anyone; since his arrival from France three months before, he complained, he had done nothing but sit around and wait.

"Wait for what?" I naturally asked.

"For my visa to America," he said. "It is all so complicated, what with the French and the Spanish and the American authorities. I spend my time running from one office to another and getting papers stamped."

I sympathized, and asked him—as anyone would—what he was going to do in America.

"I have an aviation invention that the American government is very interested in," he said. "In fact, they are very anxious for me to come over."

I pressed that question no further for the moment, but turned instead to France and asked him about conditions there. He had left, of course, before the Allied invasion. I could not help wondering how he got from France to Spain without Vichy assistance. I took the bull by the horns and said as much.

Cavaillez shrugged. "What would you have?" he said. "It was important for me to get out of France, where there is no future, and do something about this invention, which is of great significance. What could I do in France? I had already fought as a pilot until the armistice stopped everything. There was nothing more I could do for France, under the Germans. So they finally let me out. Anyway, I have never been political. This whole De Gaulle-Vichy feud in France is pointless and stupid. You cannot divide people up that way. There is much to be said both ways, although of course nobody likes the Germans. I have always hated the "Boches." But it does no good to stir up a country into such violent factions, it only creates ill feelings and chaos. The French are impossible politically anyway. The Popular Front was proof enough of that—" He then dropped a few casual remarks about "Communists and Jews not helping things any." But I did not need that addition to know that I was in the presence of a pure Vichy specimen.

The only compatriots he claimed to know in Madrid were members of the Vichy Legation, of which Pietri was minister. Of the vital, as then unrecognized De Gaullist mission in Madrid, he knew no one. He spoke highly, however, of certain members of the United States Consulate with whom he had been in contact. "They are so charming," he said, "so friendly and understanding. I hope they will not hold up my visa much longer, I am so tired of waiting in this filthy country."

A few days after my first meeting with Cavaillez, I happened to meet the young Vice-Consul of whom he had spoken. I told him about Cavaillez and said the fellow looked pure Vichy to me and hence unreliable. "How come you're giving him a visa to America?" I asked. I knew that this was the kind of question no diplomat ever answers, so the evasive reply didn't surprise me.

"We know all about him," said the young man. I said I hoped they did, and let it go at that. It is clear now that they did; it is one of the few instances in which I was compelled to admire the actions of our Foreign Service in Spain. They were giving Cavaillez a three-thousand-mile rope to hang himself with.

Not being gifted with clairvoyance, I did not then tag Cavaillez as the super-Nazi spy he turned out to be. I did, however, have acumen enough to distrust him profoundly and to want to find out more about him. His story simply did not make enough sense. I thought, in short, that I might be of use.

In August I had to go to Barcelona on an assignment, and Cavaillez and I had a farewell drink in a garden café near the Ritz.

"I shall probably have left for America before you come back to Madrid," he said, "so please let me know where I can reach you in New York so that we can meet again there." I gave him *The New Yorker*'s address. He then said:

"Tell me a little about life in America—what it costs for an apartment, how much is food, what is the best part of town to live—that sort of thing."

I advised him as well as I could. Among the questions was one that surprised me: "Can one live adequately in New York on a thousand a month?"

"Good heavens, yes," I exclaimed. "A single man can live like a lord on that." I did not ask him how he expected to have that much income. It was sufficiently surprising that an ex-officer of the French airforce could live at the Ritz in Madrid month on end. I assumed that the Vichy government was supporting him and that the American officials concerned must know about that too.

"I am looking forward enormously to my trip," said Cavaillez. "I hope to see a lot of interesting people—mostly aviation engineers, of course. Are you familiar with aviation circles at all?"

This was the first time in our many encounters that he had asked even a remotely suspicious question. "Not many," I said. "Nobody particularly important," and let it go at that.

When I got back to Madrid from Barcelona a month later, toward the end of August, the first person I meet in the lobby of the Ritz is Paul Cavaillez.

"What, you still here?" I said. He shrugged and smiled. "The usual impossible bureaucracy," he sighed. "Papers and more papers. But I am really supposed to sail in October, finally—on a Spanish boat."

"Well, that's not far off," I said. "What's holding you up?"

"Oh, there's still some document or other I need for getting on the ship at Vigo. Believe it or not, I need a German exit permit along with the American and Spanish!" I admitted the astonishment I felt. I knew the Germans were deep into the Falangist and police systems of Spain, but this seemed a little too overt to be credible. It could only mean what I did not yet feel qualified to confirm—that Paul Cavaillez was not only a Vichyite but in the active good graces of the Germans. There were men of Vichy who sincerely disliked their German masters, but Cavaillez was not one of them in spite of his protestations.

During my last days in Madrid, I, too, had to haunt the official Spanish quarters to get my exit visa and other necessary documents, and on two or three occasions Cavaillez and I went to the Seguridad building—the police center of Madrid—in the Puerta del Sol. Under this building, deep under the street, is a prison for political suspects, Spanish Republicans. I had heard enough about it to shudder every time I set foot in the Seguridad offices above it. I felt as if I were walking over graves.

The last time we visited the Seguridad was to retrieve our passports with the final stamps on them. The unshaven Falangist petty officials were as surly as ever, the air as stale, the dust as thick in the offices. About twelve of us waited in a line for our names to be called.

"Katz—German!" A shaven-headed, middle-aged man with glasses stepped to the window and was handed his passport.

"Kempinger—German!"

"Figueras—Portuguese!"

"Ahmann—German!"

"Cavaillez—French!" Cavaillez took his passport, smiling.

"García—Spanish!"

"Mannes—American!" I took my passport, with relief. When the Spaniards get your passport you wonder if you will ever see it again, particularly if you belong to an Allied nation.

We went out together into the baking sun of the Puerta del Sol, so aptly named. He was triumphant. "At last—at last!" he cried. "We must have a drink on this happy event!"

We went and had a Pernod in a big bar on the Avenida José Antonio. I had never seen the Frenchman so jubilant.

The next day I flew from Madrid to Lisbon. I was held up

by Clipper delays in Lisbon for over two weeks. When I finally left the Lisbon suburb of Estoril, where I stayed, for the Pan American base on the Tagus basin, I saw a passenger ship steaming into the broad Tagus estuary from the sea. Even at two miles I could read the name printed along its hull: SS *Magellanes*. On it was Paul Cavaillez, bound for the United States.

I had not been home in New York for more than three weeks when I received a thick letter forwarded to me by *The New Yorker*. On notepaper of the Hotel Pierre, Cavaillez wrote a lively narrative of his trip and the hope of a meeting in the near future.

We met a few days later in the Pierre bar. Cavaillez looked tanned and prosperous. When I expressed surprise at finding him established in such luxury, when the average citizen found it hard to get into any hotel, he said he had a *copain* (French for "buddy") who knew the manager well and arranged it for him. I asked him how he was getting on.

"Fine, fine," he said. "Everyone is very nice and I have already met some important men in the aviation field. I am only worried a little about the draft. It seems I may be mobilized. Just imagine," he laughed, "here I make the war in 1939 and '40, and come all the way over to America just to get caught in the army again! It will be very inconvenient for my plans, of course. I am hoping my friends in Washington can fix it somehow. It is really absurd, when I was brought over here just to present an invention of great military value to the United States experts."

He called me a week later to say that he had to go to Washington about this business of the draft, but would call me the minute he got back. After about two weeks I got a long, rueful letter from Cavaillez, postmarked Washington, to say that he had indeed been mobilized into the American Army but hoped somehow to extricate himself and would keep me advised. I did not see him again for three months.

In March he telephoned me at my home. He was demobilized at last, thank God, he said, and would I dine with him soon. He was in wonderful spirits when I did. The work was going fine, three important aeronautical engineers were very interested in his patents, he had a nice apartment at the San Carlos on Fiftieth Street, American women were beautiful if cool, life was indeed splendid. He even had some French friends out on Long Island with whom he played golf every now and then, although on the whole he found the French in New York very unsympathetic and unfriendly.

The only criticism he had against American men—those he knew, at least—was that they were so specialized in their own fields that intellectually they were very limited. That was why, he said often, it was such a pleasure to talk to someone of general interests and knowledge.

On one occasion, however, he did concentrate on shop-talk long enough to describe his invention to me. It was a device by which pilots could land their planes in darkness or in fog, and consisted in part of a method of fluorescent—"neon," he called it—triangulation. He explained that he had first worked out the idea for seaplanes landing on water at night, but that now it was extended to all aircraft. He asked me whether I would care to see his drawings and patents. I said, "Yes, with great interest," but he always managed to forget to bring them along whenever we met, and I decided not to push the issue. He did, however, show a letter he had received from the General Electric Company asking him to Schenectady to demonstrate his process. He mentioned other similar trips to other firms, and indicated that he spent a good part of his days away from New York on professional matters.

Cavaillez' conversation proved him to be a man of wide interests. He knew a good deal about music, possibly because his *amie* in Paris was a Conservatoire prize-winning pianist. He was highly intelligent on the subject of motion pictures, psychology, journalism, and even child care. He had adopted two male children in France and showed me photographs of them repeatedly. He was, like nearly all Frenchmen, very articulate on the art of love. Through all the many conversations we had, however, he kept constantly stressing the advantages of being without strong emotions. "I want to see everything objectively," he said. "It is the only way to live."

At one of our recent meetings I told him I had to leave right after dinner to go to a private Signal Corps showing of the German prison camp atrocity films. He accompanied me to their place of projection in Astoria. As I was about to go in, after showing my invitation card, I asked the attendant—on the spur of the moment—whether I could bring in a guest. The request was granted. I wanted to see how far Cavaillez' objectivity could be sustained.

Through forty uninterrupted minutes of atrocities, from Belsen to Buchenwald, the audience of journalists was frozen in silence. They seemed not even to breathe. Cavaillez' eyes never left the screen, though his face did not change in any way.

Out in the street, after the show was over, I said, "Well? How did you like those?"

He was silent for a moment. "It gives one a chill on the neck," he said, and fell silent again. A little later, he said, "They must be mad—they must be mad to do things like that. Sane people could not do that to other human beings."

We walked along a little while, not talking. "Of course," he said, "One could not help noticing that most of the faces were Jewish—in all the camps."

"There were many who were not," I said. "You know, if you starve anyone long enough, only eyes and nose are left. Eyes and nose are predominant Jewish characteristics. Nearly everyone who is starved to death might look like a Jew. Even you," I said.

For the first time since I had known him, Cavaillez looked deeply troubled. "There is something in what you say," he said in a low voice. "Eyes and nose—I never thought of that—"

I felt that the last person in the world I wanted to be with after seeing those films was Paul Cavaillez. I excused myself abruptly and went home, refusing accompaniment.

I did not think, after that evening, that he would call me again. But in a few days he did, and—more unwilling than ever but no less curious—I agreed to dine with him on a Friday night and go to a concert. He was to pick me up at my home at six forty-five.

That Friday night I was stood up. The papers Saturday morning—May 26, 1945—told me why. Paul Cavaillez had been arrested by the FBI on charges of espionage against the United States for Germany.

6.

The ghost of Mata Hari was laid (in a manner of speaking) that winter of 1945. At home I found a small boy more beautiful than ever who looked at me as if I were a stranger. No greater reminder of what I had done to him was needed.

But recognition of a pattern, once it is set, does not constitute change; however much intended. The adventurer in me would often continue to prevail, at a child's expense, over the parent.

A man would understand if not excuse. And so would an honest woman, parent or not.

• • •

The adventurer settled into a new apartment, leading a stable if not conventional life. The rhythm of love and work resumed. The latter consisted of free-lance writing for various magazines, narrations for Pathé documentaries-"This is America" series, used by the Army abroad—and the book and lyrics of a revue with music. True to form, this set off sparks in the commercial mind but failed to ignite.

By summer the adventurer had a brief but rewarding fling abroad. Condé Nast sent me to Italy with a photographer to write a series on the arts in Italy: what had happened to the writers and painters and sculptors and actors now freed from Fascism?

We concentrated chiefly on Rome and Milan, where most of them worked, but I made a brief and painful detour to Florence and the villa. I wanted to see the dear man, its devoted Italian guardian and still my friend, and take him his favorite cigarettes long denied in the war. The villa had been occupied by Canadian soldiers, he told me, and although he had done his best, he said, it was not the same. I told him I did not want to see it. With tears in our eyes, we parted.

In two weeks we saw a brilliant range of talent, from the architects and designers in Milan, to the dominant creative figures in Rome.

The writers Moravia, Ignazio Silone, Carlo Levi, Vittorini; Guttuso and Vespignani, the first already a famous painter, the second rising to prominence; sculptors Mirko and Mazzacurati; these and many others we met and photographed, aside from the ascendant film-makers, Visconti and De Sica among them, who were making history in the world as well as in Italy.

It was less surprising that these artists had emerged from the war with their vitality intact (Italian resilience and Italian compliance seem partners) than that the Italian aristocracy showed no signs of erosion.

The war took a terrible toll of Italy's poor, but the nobility lived on in their unravaged palazzi in a style unknown to even rich Americans. Fashion was booming, and the beautiful noble ladies in their ravishing clothes came clammering to be photographed for *Vogue.* It gave me a childish pleasure to tell one in particular, who had snubbed me in Florence, that our assignment covered only working artists.

As far as women were concerned, we much preferred Anna Magnani, whom we found by appointment in her hotel suite superbly tousled from what was clearly an interrupted battle of bed in the room beyond. Since my faithful colleague was homosexual (hotels could never understand our separate rooms) I envied her.

For me, however, the real excitement of this trip lay in Egypt and Palestine. I had a mandate for the former (there were Beautiful People in Egypt) and the loan of a Leica instead of a live photographer.

My week in Cairo, with excursions to Alexandria, was absorbing enough, both professionally and personally. As a base for exotic meetings the bar and terrace at Raffles was unsurpassed, and among more tangible diversions I remember fondly being joined by a Scottish engineer one day in a new kind of encounter. Total strangers, we found ourselves in an erotic contest as to who could arouse the other most by words alone.

It ended in a tie; and my craven flight.

This Egypt of twenty-five years ago I found compellingly strange and strangely stifling: a mixture of beauty and ugliness as extreme as the pyramids and the worm-infested fellaheen. I was drawn to Egypt and yet frightened by it. It seemed lost in time, drugged by the weight of its past yet dragooned by the forces of hate into the present.

As for Palestine, I was warned not to go there, then in '46. The King David Hotel had just been blown up, the Stern

Gang was on the rampage, and General Cassels' British forces were everywhere.

I flew as planned, however, secure in my press-card from *The New Yorker* clipped to my passport. The ten days there, based in a Jerusalem hotel with a cluster of correspondents (including the handsome young New York *Times* reporter, Clifton Daniel) were, to say the least, shaking. Aside from the beauty of the land itself and the constant hallucination of Christ, two events still cling.

One was a ride in General Cassels' Jeep (how I got there I do not know, although he asked me) from Jerusalem to Haifa during which, for the first and I hope my last time, bullets from unseen sources kept whistling past our heads.

The other was going out on a small boat from Haifa harbor to meet a ship full of survivors from refugee camps in Europe. I shall never forget two things. Alongside the hull, the smell from the black portholes just above our heads was overpoweringly foul: the breath of a thousand latrines and a hundred hours of sweat. And finally, coming down the gang-plank to the tender nearby, the faces of the near-dead.

When some of them smiled, it became unbearable.

• • •

Back home, I free-lanced again (including an indepth first-hand report on Harlem as a dangerous focus of explosion, which the American Mercury ordered and then rejected as "proving nothing"), and finally accepted an offer from Condé Nast, Inc. as feature editor on *Glamour*. I liked my colleagues and knew my job, which they agreed to limit to one year at my request. I didn't want to fall into that world again as a way of life.

Glamour, moreover, was much less pretentious and social

than *Vogue;* geared to young women but not yet catering to the cult of youth.

By 1947 the old exploring urge rose up again: this time for new places of the mind, new forms of expression. I spent most of the following year writing a novel and, for once, finishing it. Called *Message From a Stranger,* it was based on a theory of immortality in which the dead resume their conscious identities at those moments when the living think of them. The story was narrated by the leading character: a woman who died in the first chapter; indeed on the first page.

Viking Press published it in 1948. And although most critics either ignored it or treated it—with tolerant deprecation—as a lending-library book (for women of course), it was taken by the Fiction Book Club, reprinted for four more years in paperback (Dell and Crowell-Collier) and ultimately sold 230,000 copies.

In due course a well-known Hollywood movie-maker bought it and later abandoned it for reasons too typical to warrant mention. By then, however, my ego was restored less by the royalties than by the enormous amount of mail from strangers all over the country who seemed sustained by the book and what it meant. It was the first experience for me in direct communication on a large scale, and made me both humble and exalted. I understood then, more clearly than ever, why my father had been happier conducting free concerts for thousands of "ordinary" people a night in the Metropolitan Museum than for the paying elite in concert halls. The crowds, mostly poor and middle class, came from all over the city simply for music. There were no big "names." Those who could find the base of a statue to lean against sat on the floor. The rest stood for nearly two hours listening to symphonic classics and the buoyant waltzes of Johann Strauss which my father loved to play as a final fillip.

There were no critics to tell them the tempo was wrong. (It was not.)

7.

Since the wartime years a serious liaison had been formed which in time superseded all other diversions. The man was an RAF officer and a test pilot: an arduous job that took him not only back and forth from England but to the major centers of aircraft production in this country and the airfields where he tested U.S. prototypes of combat planes for prospective use in Britain. There were frequent separations during all six years which, added to personal complications, made any permanent relation unfeasible until 1948. Then, when he was appointed Civil Air Attaché to the British Embassy in Washington, we married and made our life for the next four years in a Georgetown house.

(Why, after seven years—again—and two lost marriages? What drove the adventuring ghost again into the constraints of wedlock and habit and security?)

Silly questions, Wohleben. You grow to prefer one man

above others, you weary again of brief encounters, you long for sustaining companionship, you think of a son in need of a man in the home: you want to hold hands, be double against the world.

(You never mentioned love. What about love?)

What about love? Of course you are in love—or believe you are. Good God, Wohleben, this ghost was a woman needing a man. What more do you want?

(The truth. She lost her nerve, didn't she? Couldn't go it alone?)

All right then, the hermaphrodite became a woman. Everyone was relieved, especially women. Her adventuring ghost was a disturbing one. Wives would say how wonderful it was to be free, or what a glamorous life you lead, or you always have your work; or if *I* weren't married I'd be a writer too. But they knew they had something I didn't have and comforted themselves with a twinge of pity. What man would be brave enough to take me on?

I got the message: damn few. Out of the dozens of men I had known quite well, only three wanted me as a wife: the three I married.

Gratitude played a great part. For so long the litany had echoed in my mind, tolling the failure in love of the stronger woman.

"Well, let's face it, it's very tough on the male ego. No man wants to compete. No man wants a woman with a superior mind (talent, job, education, character, skill) around."

I had come to believe it. But what could I do? The ghosts had merged into a reality, complex as it was. The humble woman praying for love inside the crusader brandishing a sword.

Many years later I described myself in a speech as trying

to be half Joan of Arc and half femme fatale: part of the time on the back of a horse in armor, and part flat on my back without it (the armor, not the horse).

In between, to recuperate, the marital fortress with the drawbridge up and contented fires burning in the hearth.

This time the fortress, built on deep affection and respect, repelled all invasions for over fifteen years. I became domesticated, discreet, socially housebroken, and more tolerant. I even lowered my voice and tried to temper (not always successfully) my natural ebullience or vehemence, as the case might be. I deferred to my husband's superior knowledge in many fields, and even in mine tried never to dominate the general scene. These were on the whole very happy and fruitful years. And I think I made a fairly good wife.

Friends were relieved, using the word "mellowed": I had joined the group at last.

• • •

In some ways, yes. During the four years in Washington I felt it incumbent not to write anything which might embarrass my husband in his embassy job. That eliminated Washington and its only industry, politics, it eliminated interviews with important persons, foreign or national, and in so doing left me few alternatives beyond superficial journalism or fiction.

The diplomatic-social scene in Washington, which fascinated me, was marvelous material for a running commentary with no holds barred; but this, of course, was out. As for fiction, in spite of the comforting sales of *Message,* I found it hard to focus imagination on anything deeply and long enough in a life, delightful as it was, which added the functions of hostess, mother, and stepmother to the normal pleasures and distractions of Washington life.

Yet even these and a son now old enough to bus to his Maryland school and back left a void which had to be filled: on paper, alone. Eventually I thought I had come on a theme worthy of the long pull of a novel, and spent several hours a day involved in it.

After a hundred pages I knew it wouldn't work, and so did my agent. The remaining time in Washington was largely fallow in writing if not in observing. Wisely I gave myself over just to being.

• • •

Nineteen fifty-two meant, of course, the end of Truman and the beginning of Eisenhower. It also meant the end of my husband's special appointment to the embassy (he was not a Foreign Office career diplomat) and the return to New York as the U.S. representative of a British aircraft corporation.

Leaving a Republican capital was no wrench. Leaving the Washington of our Georgetown house and the people we loved was hard, particularly for him. A sensitive man with no taste for the fierce competitive wars of big business and no love for New York's own special ferocity, the move filled him with apprehensions.

These were at least partly allayed by an apartment found in the old Dakota, with all its windows facing the blessed oasis of Central Park and the towers beyond.

As for the job, barring the cockpit which all crack pilots would rather inhabit, it promised at least to call on his manifold expertise in aircraft specifications, markets, and needs in a country he now knew well.

For me, of course, Manhattan was a shot in the arm and a call *to* arms. The old beat began to drum in my head again, and I started to polish my saddle and lance.

My horse turned out to be a fairly new magazine called *The Reporter,* its liberal pennant having been won by a sharp and comprehensively documented attack—the first—on the China Lobby.

I was introduced to its editor Max Ascoli at a cocktail party in 1952 in an elegant apartment overlooking the East River. He was a big man with a daunting dictatorial face, thick glasses, and an even thicker Italian accent. He was disarmingly polite and attentive, he asked me what I wanted to do, I told him what I wanted to do, and that was that. I was to write a regular column on television, twice a month, on the clear understanding that I would not submit any copy until I had looked at the tube for several weeks.

This was the fortuitous beginning of a twelve-year job on *The Reporter* as staff writer: a term that included theater and TV criticism, straight reporting, and satirical sketches, as well as political satire in verse under the name of Sec.

In 1963 I left, or was fired from, *The Reporter.* I could no longer hide my deep political differences from my editor, and was not—like most of his writers—permitted to air them, even in the doggerel of Sec. Ascoli had grown increasingly committed to Johnson and the Vietnam war, increasingly hostile to the Kennedys. Seeing himself as the only truly rational liberal voice in America he resented or denigrated those, especially Adlai Stevenson, who emerged as its favored symbols. In Europe, moreover, the only statesmen he listened to with respect and credence were De Gaulle and Adenauer. As one of the most premature of the anti-Fascists in his native Italy, his credentials for being an American anti-Communist were impeccable. He had fought, bravely and at personal risk, against tyranny.

Yet I saw *The Reporter* turn more and more from the very

awareness that had made it for so long an expression of new political thinking and reporting that answered a growing need in intelligent Americans. By now it was edging predictably, and ironically, to the right, prodded by Ascoli's brilliantly abstract intelligence; abstract in that it seemed sometimes to blunt his sensitivity to human response.

Whatever the deep political divisions there were then between Ascoli and myself, he was—and still is—a loyal and valued friend. He was also not only a very good editor but the only editor who has ever given me the freedom, the range, and the confidence to write as I chose and to print it—regularly, for twelve years.

And it was because of this confidence, this regularity of exposure, moreover, that I did much of my best writing. Geniuses may be able to produce best by self-motivation; but most writers function best on demand. And the worst that can happen to a writer (or man, or woman) is not to be wanted.

• • •

On the home front, all seemed quiet. Security in the hearth; security in work. Both productive for man and woman, both enjoyable. It seemed, in short, that explorer-wife could live together, and with another, in peace, even if peace was then denied to the third of our family by a difficult adolescence: the trial of so many young, but for which I felt a heavy responsibility.

In 1953, however, the adventurer stirred again, impelled by a nagging residue from the war.

In 1945, right after the collapse and defeat of the Nazi Reich, my brother had called me early one morning at our apartment.

"Have you seen the *Times* yet?"

"No. Not yet. Why?"

"Look at the lower right of the first page . . ."

I grabbed the paper and saw a paragraph date-lined London which reported a short-wave item from Germany allegedly monitored by the BBC. It said that after the capture of Heinrich Himmler a certain Colonel von R., his deputy, was left in command.

"My God, no. . . . Heinz?" I said.

"Must be," said my brother. "Horrible, isn't it?"

We had a habit of sharing the agonies of catastrophe: the Los Alamos bomb, Hiroshima, unspeakable acts. And now this very small, but intensely personal thing. A second-cousin, a man of our mother's blood and our own, presumably part of this horror.

Actually, all ties with our German relatives had been cut before World War II when some of their letters had indicated a growing feeling for German "rebirth" through Hitler. Affection for one remarkable and free-spirited older cousin, a retired teacher, survived this schism, but my mother was otherwise violent in her rejection.

My last sight of our junker forebears was at a clan gathering at a Baltic seaport in 1921, a side excursion from one of my parents' summer tours. They were all together in their modest house for the yearly celebration. My rosy sweet old great-uncle with his sweeping white mustache and warm brown eyes wore the *feldgrau* uniform, the medals, and the peaked helmet (*Pickelhaube*) of the General he was in 1914 (he had fought as a youth in the war of 1870). One of his stalwart sons wore his naval uniform as a U-boat commander in 1914–18, the women relatives were in their festive best. One brother, a tea planter in Java, was absent.

A third brother, tall and handsome, with dueling scars on

his cheeks, wore no uniform then. Later, however, he took us to see a factory hidden in a forest where the pretext was the manufacture of gliders, but where, in direct defiance of the Allied commission, plane engines were being produced.

But the party that night was a surge of toasts, a banquet of rich food, and resounding *a cappella* song in which all our relatives joined with the perfect pitch and beautiful full true voices which seemed part of the German and certainly of our family's heritage. Between some martial choruses, young and old sang Schubert, Bach, Brahms. I remember that only my Australian great-aunt, the General's wife, was too shy to join in.

She and the other women worried a great deal about my thinness and pallor. Repeatedly they forced food on me although my mother kept telling them I was as strong as a horse and not the pink-cheek type.

The next morning my great-uncle, still in his feldgrau cape, took me for a walk along the esplanade by the sullen gray northern sea. When we turned right, he would bellow "Rechts!" when we turned left, "Links!" making military turns which I copied, laughing with him.

Although this group geniality overlaid the strong pan-Germanism which my parents and brother so feared and hated, its natural evolvement into Nazism twenty years later should not have surprised us. They were born and trained to be patriots and to love authority, and Bismarck was then their idol.

So when I found myself in Berlin in 1932, then single and on assignment, but also to meet C. again, I found the atmosphere heavily sinister, very much like that sultry leaden pause before a storm. Innocent still in my twenties, I was shocked by the sexual displays in the night clubs, incredulous that the bosomy blondes in slithering gowns who were dancing with men were men themselves.

The only healthy manifestation (aside from the country beauty), I felt, was the fight for survival of the Social Democrats, mostly workers. An English correspondent smuggled me into one of their basement meetings, and I found them and what they said both brave and right. After several speeches and rounds of beer I was introduced as an American writer and found myself trying to answer a barrage of questions, in German of course, about the situation of the worker in America. Due to the political retardation mentioned earlier in these pages, I was appallingly ignorant of union structure, specific wage scales for specific work, and labor legislation. I could, however, tell them the way certain kinds of workers in certain areas lived. What their houses were like, what they paid for their cars and clothes, and so on. They seemed both incredulous and interested.

But my cousin in Hamburg, where my job then took me, was something else. Still tall and handsome with his dueling credentials, he was then, as a long-time flyer, Captain of the Air Police of this city, the husband of the standard meek German wife and the father of a growing brood. Although he was highly intelligent, we had little to talk about except family news. But the strut in his voice, the sense of a power soon to be his and that of Germany were unmistakable and chilling.

In a lighter moment I chided him, smiling, about the aggressive manner of some of his countrymen: I had been accosted on the street and in hotel corridors; disturbingly.

He looked at me seriously and coldly and said, "What do you expect, fixing yourself up like that?"

I was dressed as any middle-class city woman would be:

simple store-bought clothes, good shoes, silk stockings. He looked at my legs and lipstick: like a whore, he meant.

Nine years later he became an obsesssion of mine, to be tracked down. In every smuggled OKW report, in every intercepted press radio message from Germany, in every list of military or diplomatic personnel, here or abroad, I looked for his name. In Spain and Portugal I checked with Allied sources as well as our own for any trace.

None was found. In 1953 I persuaded a publisher to advance me the needed money to go to Germany and finish the story.

What I found in Hamburg was a story of decimation. Most of the men of the family killed or executed, most of the women uprooted, one of them driven to madness before death.

His daughters, the youngest barely eight, were raised in a modest apartment by the great-aunt who never wanted Hitler's Reich from the start. For years a teacher of English in private schools, deeply educated in the humanities and the beauty of reason, she felt the barbaric doom that awaited both in the form of their fuehrer.

My last night in Hamburg then, the child of the man I was hunting kneeled at her bed and prayed for him. His picture was on the wall right over the bed, in the uniform—blaze on the collar, high peaked cap and all—of his rank and trade.

Yet all that his family knew of him was that he never came back (of course they kept track of all prisoner trains from the East) and that he had been "de-nazified" in absentia by an Allied court.

In Berlin I spent my time shuttling between East and West, sniffing his trail. It was not considered the safest excursion, and I admitted to being uncomfortable passing the border guards and walking the bleak and ugly Stalin Allee under the watchful eyes of the youthful *Vopo.* The sight of the death bunkers and the now-shabby Adlon made me shudder.

For all my efforts, contacts, and risks, I learned only this: When the Russians caught up with him, he was taken with the others to the detention camp at Lichterfelde, once the imperial training school for Army cadets. Someone who saw him there described him accurately; as clearly a "gentleman" who had given his overcoat to a chilled fellow prisoner.

He was then taken by train to Lubyanka prison in Moscow. It is unnecessary to explain why two subsequent visits to that city for other purposes were, in this particular search, counter productive.

End of trail. Abort of book. Perhaps it was just as well. The BBC report may have erred. And if it were true, the immense national guilt of which this man seemed a part is no part of his children, living and working in a new Germany or elsewhere. My German blood joined with the Jew had given me music and strength, and the world great men. The ancient crest with the rampant stags is still on my wall.

• • •

Why mention all this? Partly, of course, to show that the explorer was not buried in the wife. Partly to suggest that an aggressive reporter might have come up with more. That is why, I imagine, I have not been considered a journalist. I find it hard to bring my peripheral vision into a single focus, to blot out pervasive intangibles, human factors bearing only partially on the main issue.

Whether covering a convention or UN sessions or a trial or a personage, I have watched my fellow reporters in dogged pursuit of facts, in the relentless collaring and questioning of every and any possible useful source; watched them knowing that I should be doing so too.

God knows I observe, I listen, I even take notes. But some fundamental shyness prevents me from forcing myself on preoccupied statesmen in the midst of crisis, from asking the mother of a psychotic boy on trial for murder how he got that way, from joining the crush around a celebrity. I marvel at the tenacity of women reporters, often more skilled in aggression even than men. But my mind nibbles constantly at meaning, asking why instead of where or when, reading faces and gestures, feeling the contours of mood, examining objects in a room or street, wondering how a senator makes love or whether his wife enjoys it.

No editors called this journalism until Norman Mailer came along to prove that the peripheral all-encompassing mind and eye came closer to truth than the single track of fact.

But then, didn't I suggest that two essential elements of talent were timing—and arrogance? The mainsprings, too, of the champion athlete.

• • •

Some hurdles I have jumped, to be sure, even on that strange unresolved German trip.

One Hamburg evening was spent in the company of a few men connected wtih Radio Free Europe. There was plenty to drink and talk about until one of them mentioned a street of prostitutes, well known, not far away, where the women sat behind glass-fronted façades for clear inspection and choice. Both ends of the mews were guarded, they said, and no women permitted. One of them added that Brahms had lived on this street in his youth.

They suggested a visit: one newcomer had not seen it. They would drop me off at my hotel, and then proceed.

They would not, I said. I had never seen this kind of thing, I had to see it, and it was imperative I find where my beloved Brahms once lived.

I was slim enough then, it evolved, to get into a suit of my host's, with shirt and tie. I washed off my lipstick and pushed my hair under the soft hat of another man. The effect in the mirror was ineffably decadent, I thought, but the men (now in the spirit) assured me I would get by if I kept my trap shut and learned to move like a man. I should watch them, they said.

So after my lesson in walking like a man, we were off. A policeman was at the mouth of the mews and my host, known to him, identified me as a visiting friend from abroad. We went in and sauntered slowly down the street.

There they sat, brightly lit, in the ground floors of the German equivalent of our brownstone rows ("Store-Front Whores?"). All shapes, all sizes, fully dressed. Most of them, I guess, over thirty, and then some. Some beckoned vivaciously, other feigned indifference. Wandering back and forth, I was sad and uncomfortable. The joke had worn off and Brahms had receded already. My comrade would ask me: this one? this one? I shrugged, then finally—and fearfully—nodded yes.

The woman was dark-haired, with an interesting Latin face. She knew my companion, it seemed, they greeted each other. She looked at me with a flick of suspicion. My companion quickly assured her I was all right. We wanted a little chat and then . . .

They bantered about time and price while I squirmed, my hat pulled down over my far from virile face, my mouth firmly closed. She gave me one more glance and said, "There's something funny going on, isn't there?" He said, not at all, my friend doesn't speak German, and so on. She muttered something about not being in the bargain, she didn't like tricks, she had plenty of other fish to fry, and so forth.

I finally pressed my knee firmly against my companion's, emitting signals of distress from my shadowed eyes. He stood up with a hearty laugh and took out his wallet. "Well, Rita," he said taking out some bills, "thanks for the visit. We're off to a party anyway. Good luck!"

Her hand reached for the bills but her eyes never left my face. "Some friend," she muttered, as we went out.

It wasn't much of a joke.

• • •

But these were among the few departures alone during the next decade. What I saw and wrote of was mainly of my own country during the Eisenhower and Joe McCarthy years. The political torpor in the White House notwithstanding, there was plenty to write about and rage against, most of which appeared regularly in *The Reporter,* intermittently in other publications, and much of it in two books of essays *More in Anger* and *But Will It Sell?,* one volume of satirical poems called *Subverse,* and in *The New York I Know,* a long deep look at the city I loved and hated which—twelve years ago—outlined its ultimate strangulation and decay while psalming its beauties. This sank without trace.

Though neither success nor failure affected the balance of our domestic life (except in the alternating moods which my husband gracefully endured), I was consistently troubled that my sporadic exposure might in some way diminish him or his feelings about himself. I might be aggressive in print, on air, or in public debate. But I have never in life sought to dominate or reduce a human being close to me. It would be inconceivable to me, in fact, to resent a husband's success if he were loved.

Yet such is the pattern of a male-dominated society that whispers of its surrounding chorus—watching, waiting—continued to reach my inner ear: (It must be tough for a man to be married to her . . . I must say, *I* couldn't take it . . . It's all very well to have a career and all that, but a woman's . . . Poor man, he's awfully good about it, but . . .)

And then, the trips. (*I* wouldn't leave a man for three weeks if I really cared. If I were he, I don't think I'd take it . . .)

But if the husband leaves for three weeks, well, that's part of his business. The wife is alone, but what of it? And if a man makes a public success, how blessed the woman!

(What is your goal in life, Mrs. President? Why, to make my husband happy!) What man in his right mind would say the equivalent? Pleasure, yes. Privilege, maybe. But reason for *being?*

For a woman to apologize for success is as pointless as for a man to apologize for failure. One is as one is, and the love that can't encompass both is a poor sort of love.

The wind is blowing at last in another direction, and the whispers of an outdated concept of life will be soon out of range. Among creative people it barely exists. Men and women who build internal and separate lives recognize in each other the urgency of this need and respect its power. Whose talent is more or less is not the point: the validity is.

But for some years then I had straddled two worlds: of artists on one hand, of business and convention on the other. I tried very hard to convince the latter, for the sake of the marriage, that the hermaphrodite, the wanton, the exhibitionist, were dead—superseded by the tractable mellowed wife.

The announcement of their demise was premature, let alone false.

• • •

The result of this tractability affected the woman more than the writer. When a relationship shifts from the invigorating tensions of love to the calms of companionship and habit, her attraction wanes. The woman resigns herself to the progressive muting of passion inevitable, she tells herself, after years of marriage. Inevitably, too, the resignation begins to slacken flesh as well as hope. And when this woman sees herself in the mirror or in photographs and tells herself "That is Over," the antennae of others and certainly of men receive it loud and clear. The state of being successfully male or female, as all must know, is based as much on love of self as love of others. Neither is productive without the other. And the moment a woman fails to love herself—loses her athlete's nerve—she is not loved, or at least, less loved, as a woman.

The adventuring body submits; the mind does not. I counted the sum of my blessings: comradeship, friends, intermittent achievement, a life of many pleasures—never dull. Nature and food and drink and encounters and travels. So much luckier than most, what else could I want?

I could escape this confrontation, this sad resolve, by running from it.

In 1960 I was asked by a major network to go to the Soviet Union and write a report on the state of their mass communications—chiefly television. To avoid complications (our newsmen had troubles enough there) I was to go as a tourist and independent journalist. An apprehensive husband saw me off in London on an Aeroflot propjet to Moscow.

So much has been written about the Soviet Union that no further descriptions of it seem warranted here. I spent three lonely, intensely interesting but frustrating weeks, partly in Moscow, partly in Leningrad, and came home with a report which was later adapted for a piece in *The New York Times Magazine*.

The gist of it was that their television then, ten years ago, was primitive by our terms, very limited, tightly controlled, of course, by the state and—except for music and dance—very dull. Yet the directors of operations I interviewed in both cities gave the same answer to the question: "What do you really think television is for?"

"To make better people," they said, with the simple amazement of people asked "What do you really think food is for?"

I could hear the derisive chuckles of network presidents in New York.

• • •

The Reporter was not the whole of my professional life during the fifties.

My first real exposure on television came with Chet Huntley's first year as anchorman on NBC-TV news. Having seen my essays in the magazine, he and his producer Reuven Frank suggested I contribute a short commentary on their evening news program once a week.

This I did, with alacrity, garnering over a number of weeks a mixed but copious mail. Then—partly because of this, partly to eliminate any distractions from the Huntley-Brinkley team, which was to be NBC's greatest asset for years—I was politely jettisoned. This became a familiar pattern through subsequent years: the price of an independence which made it impossible for me to tailor my comments, on air or in print, for mass acceptability. The sudden termination of regular commentaries on ABC-TV in the sixties, in my case at least, was familiar proof of network aversion to controversial speakers who were not, alas, either sex objects, entertainers, or men.

Yet in '59 Channel 5 gave me a weekly talk-interview program which consisted of a half hour with some distinguished man or woman as guest in which I was given maximum freedom. Although I had no conception of how to dress for television and appeared on screen looking like a hefty and raddled Roman matron, the series drew large and largely appreciative mail and I was asked to continue for another thirteen weeks. With my usual conspicuous talent for missing a main chance, I declined. The reason was simple to me if not to others. I had found that the weekly program had become a daily absorption at the expense of thinking and writing, and I did not want to become a "television personality." I had seen others locked into this particular public prison, plush as it was, and I wanted out. The world beyond was still too desirable.

• • •

Yet subsequent trips, to Europe and later across this country for specific purposes which gave me valid reasons for flight and refreshment, for new contexts in which I could not brood on private fears, were still only brief interruptions in my domestic and working life in New York.

After I left *The Reporter* in 1963 I began to fight my own battles in print and on air wherever I could be seen and heard. Cartons of copies and clippings attest to speeches ranging from population control to repeal of abortion laws, from urban blight to the cults of non-art, from abolishment of the draft to environmental disaster, before these had entered the public consciousness as "acceptable" issues. The need to liberate women and men from the social stereotypes that were crippling them both was a constant cry even before *The Feminine Mystique* and NOW. So was the built-in death of the consumer culture that enforced these myths. And since 1965 the abomination of the war in Vietnam and our pursuit of it ran through speeches and commentaries (mainly on public television) long before the public massings of protest in which I sometimes found myself—for the first time and in real trepidation—talking from sound-trucks or platforms to crowds in streets.

On home base I spoke to colleges, medical groups, suburban forums, business conventions, religious organizations, even to members of Congress. In 1965 I was called by the counsel for Senator Hart's committee as the first witness to testify to deceptive packaging of foods: outraged consumer, now, as well as writer.

As for articles, monthly pieces for *McCall's* ranged far and wide during 1967 and the same magazine allowed me to indulge my fascination for movies in a column of film reviews during 1968. In between all this, I appeared intermittently in publications as diverse as *TV Guide, Vogue,* the *New Republic, The National Observer,* the New York *Times, Newsday,* and in syndicated material for national newspaper supplements.

There is a conspicuous absence above of the loftier magazines devoted to markedly intellectual tastes, and of the newer publications so dedicated to the Relevance of Now that my age alone would disqualify me, let alone my elitist soul.

I have had to accept this gracefully, aware in the first instance that my intellect is deficient and in the second that my writing is, alas, proficient, meaning what it says. In an age of symbolic allusion and treasured confusion, this spells death.

If I can hang on long enough, however, a public may rise, craving to understand what is said to them without radar equipment, monumental effort, or the abdication of judgment so essential to the condition of being With It.

In 1964 I spent a summer month in Salzburg, Austria, as one of four Americans lecturing at the Seminar for American Studies of Schloss Leopoldskron. Our audience was a group of Fellows from all over Europe, hand-picked for scholarships in various fields. Our area concerned social conditions in the United States.

The subject assigned to me had been race relations, despite my demur on the basis of second-hand knowledge. I had, to be sure, spent previous months reading every book and paper and report I could and talking to Negroes (then so-called, and then leaders) in various fields, but conveying the right conclusions to foreign ears when we ourselves were already foundering in the growing tumult, was the toughest assignment I ever hope to take.

As in all such experiences, I learned the most. "When in doubt, do" still worked.

It worked again in another visit to the U.S.S.R. in 1966, on a press junket, very brief, and marred by sickness. But my curiosity about this enormous nation and a real affection for its beleaguered people managed again to supersede—however temporarily—an aversion to the drabness of daily Soviet life and a much deeper one to the deadly weight of the Kremlin leadership.

Solzhenitsyn and his countrymen are the redeemers. Or would be if they ever got the chance.

From '64 onward, however, these trips abroad were more flight than adventure. Wohleben still lurked inside, but beside him was a woman aware not only that her absences caused no pain, that indeed they relieved an atmosphere at home now dense with unspoken words and unavowed feelings.

Since '63 only the outer shell of this long good marriage remained; fragile and cracked. The weekend of John Kennedy's assassination, alone for the hours of day and night before the television set, all loss, all sorrow merged in a merciless vigil of grief: for the shattered President in his coffin, for the nation, the world, and the murder of hope. The funeral drums beat for us all.

Ironically, in the previous spring a picture story in *Life* showed a ravaged woman playing at domesticity when she was not walking into the sea-wind on a lonely beach: her spirit's domain. It was the picture of a large ghost, sick with rejection while she acted happy-home-with-handsome-husband. Unhorsed; only the mind's lance able to function at all. I have never been able to fight for what has been withheld, nor could I ever understand women who did.

But I was (in that story) at least able to laugh with one of my loves. The people on *Life* knew my peculiar passion for lions and set up a session with the circus at Madison Square Garden to photograph me with a litter of cubs. Ten years before I had held a very heavy six-months-old-lion on my lap in the Berlin Tiergarten. But these cubs still mewled and crawled on my knees and around my neck, their huge paws clinging and climbing, their whiskers tickling my chin. I stroked them while the camera clicked. Their claws hurt, but it was worth it to hold them close.

Afterward I walked up in the late spring sun toward home. The joy of the cubs wore off, the numbness set in. I noticed that people were looking at me strangely, but thought maybe that my jacket was torn or my face dirty; and didn't care.

When I got home I looked in the mirror and saw that my neck was red with blood, soaking into my blouse. But it didn't matter. Nothing much mattered.

And in the summer of 1964 when the brother I loved died suddenly, it mattered even less.

He was buried in the small cemetery at Chilmark, on Martha's Vineyard, which had been his summer home for many years and which he so loved.

On a gray and windy day, in the presence of his widow, his daughter, and his closest friends, these words were said of him:

"Here rests—at last—a man who knew little peace except in music, on his boat alone, or in the company of those who loved and understood him.

"Leopold was a universal man—as much at home with the structure of the atom as with the form of a fugue: a man of limitless intelligence, a playful wit, and a deeply generous spirit. He gave far more to the world than he received from it.

"Yet this man of great resources was not only totally free of the competitive spirit which this brutal time seems to demand for survival—he was almost painfully modest. Although we who loved him knew him to be so much better than most of us, he himself thought he was never good enough."

These and a few more were the most difficult words his sister ever had to speak.

• • •

In time, of course, I would rediscover the full sustaining bounty of friends and lovers.

Until then, resignation: devouring, leaden, a sickness of body as well as of mind. A time before it was time when

I turned on myself perversely in a sonnet sequence *On One Theme:*

1.

This tragedy, so common, has its being
In countless rooms before a looking glass;
The villain, age; the victim, woman seeing
For the first time her youth and beauty pass.
The action lives in the soliloquy
Addressed by her to her own heavy heart
As, humbled there, she whispers: look at me
And see the web of dissolution start.
Look at this drying mouth and dying skin,
This dimming eye, this dulling, brittle hair;
Look at the wavering contour of the chin;
Inspect them. Yesterday they were not there.
Yesterday I was young; and now I know
Beyond deceit, I am no longer so.

2.

Beyond deceit, beyond the oils and creams
So advertised to arrest the hour hand,
I now push off the layers of my dreams
And in a harsh light, unassisted, stand;
Admitting that by no bloom of skin or hair,
No subtle distillation of the flesh,
Will he be drawn to me. He will be there
Held only by the gentle, intricate mesh
Woven by our two lives. And from now on
I can expect no ardent semaphore
From eyes across a room. Those days are gone,
And with enchantment, will return no more.
No more, she says. So I must put aside
The ignominious remnants of my pride.

3.

And then in this, as in so many a room,
The humbled woman will lift up her head
And hold her features so that they assume
The quality of beauty she thought dead;
And for a time this private agony
Is muted by illusion: that in some lights,
Some gowns, some movements and attitudes, that she
Is still unchanged. But soon the heart indicts
What mind imagined, and she is left with fear;
Until a voice calls or a call demands,
And she is needed, she is needed here,
And she goes swiftly, holding out her hands,
Holding them out; in her solicitude
With an inalterable beauty now imbued.

8.

And so it transpired. The beauty was altered but the hand and heart were held out, freely. In time I would find that some men could still love me as I loved them: lightly, fondly, or lustily, with no claims. I still look at men of any age with an ageless eye, even when I know that the balance of reciprocation is heavily weighted otherwise.

The writer, however, was not doing so well:

The phone has hardly rung all day. It may have something to do with the strike—people not on the job—but I suspect it is a continuation of this eerie silence that seems to have descended on me for months now. But it doesn't worry me as much as it did before, possibly because I feel better now that the undulant fever has finally gone, possibly because I am determined to pull myself out of what appears to be an occupational slump by fresh efforts and energy.

Remembering back five years, I believe I had thought that an honest daily journal, recording in detail one year in the life of this city and this nation in this time might make a book. I liked the flexibility of the form, finding letters and diaries close to the moment often more revealing than tempered (and tampered) afterthought.

"Tempered" was clearly not the word for scattered passages spurred by the transport strike that year and month; and a union leader:

He has the kind of face that has never tasted pleasure: slit mouth, inverted U, that could never have kissed well or eaten subtly. An old man's joyless mouth, arrogant and ignorant. Everything that is bad with old-time Irish puritan Catholicism is in him. Here is the anti-mind, anti-body, anti-love, anti-law brawler, canny as they come, fanatic as they go. And senile now.

January 1966

Went to a party last night chock-full of In-People: all the little soft-spoken fags who tell women what to wear and how to do their hair, all the little girls in play clothes, with no buttocks and a tangle of hair, and a sprinkling of famous faces—commentators and comics and extremely successful people. Most of them knew each other with that easy fraternity of equals which always makes me feel like the outsider—not quite up to it, or them. It is always my fate too to be exposed to the fashion-arbiters when my hair is bedraggled and my clothes clearly not designed by any of them.

There were nice people, among them a professor at UCLA, who didn't Belong either, but I can't say that I had a happy time. Every second person seemed to be taking pictures, which I find very disconcerting at a private party, and I spent my time either dodging the lens or sucking my stomach in, both exhausting exercises. Nearly all snapshots make me look either like a disheveled harridan or an aging Juno. Possibly I am both, but don't care to know it.

• • •

Went to my work room to start the review of Jean Stafford's book on Lee Oswald's mother, but couldn't get down to it because this is one of those days when I am suffused with an undirected sensuality—sexuality, if you will—that is very distracting. The body is so conscious of itself—in a pleasing way—that the mind is muffled. I can well understand why men in this state of general and unfocused desire are not fussy about the woman who can receive—and expunge—it. It has nothing to do with love and everything to do with need: a matter of heat and skin and touch and release, a very simple and healthy joy.

Although, as I said, this feeling is not very productive of writing, I am grateful to it for temporarily blotting out the terrible sense of professional inadequacy that has pulled me low all this fall. The rash of rejections now makes me expect rejection. Even when an editor accepts a piece, I don't expect to see it in print. What has happened? Possibly the simple fact that a lot of people, most of them young, write a lot better—or more freshly, more pungently, more topically. What have I got to give except communicable prose and, I think, some sense? Not enough, I expect. I mean that this is not enough now. I must find some way to break through, but how?

What's this? Dug up from some forgotten box. Why kept? After four books and a continuous flow of articles, why back to an earlier ghost who talked to herself because nobody else would listen?

The old communicable loss of nerve again. Two years alone, and now divorced, the blow to the woman still paralyzed the writer.

The mark of genius, perhaps, is to separate these things. Or if not separate, then to translate such pains and losses into work itself and thereby be free of them. The genius may not be sure of his worth in specific works. But he (always "he") is sure enough of his whole and ultimate worth to submerge purely human concerns for the sake of it.

Illness of body or mind (his own) can of course reduce his power. Rejection never.

• • •

Wohleben: What happened to you . . . or rather, to me? You sound all woman, for God's sake!

Me: The sonnets you mean? Oh well, maybe . . . Dependent, self-pitying . . .

W: Yes, but then all this business about the male "genius" not feeling rejection, only the poor damn paralyzed female writer. How do you think *I* feel when I fall on my face?

M: Just that you've slipped. Not been kicked.

W: Look. There's something you're not saying, something you're scared to say.

M: Scared? To *you?*

W: Didn't you really want all along to be me—all man?

M: No, my interior campanion, I did not. It is a marvelous thing to be physically a woman if only to know the marvels of a man. I love them too much to be one of them. I thought I made that clear to you (and Freud) when I first saw what my brother had and did not envy it. Later, as you well know, I grew to worship your vital member.

W: As *you* well know, that is not all there is to a man. Surely you envied some freedoms that were mine?

M: Yes. I did. Although if I were young *now* I might have them too.

For years, in fact, I have searched myself for signs of paranoia, the convenient excuse to blame my gender for what failures I've had.

W: Excuse? Come on now, you know the odds.

M: Yes, I do. The main and only reason I wished I'd been a man was to have a wife. Look around, for God's sake, W., and wonder how many of our conspicuously creative males could produce so consistently and well without a woman (wife, secretary, companion) to keep their home a haven and the world away from the door.

What about us? Married, even single, we have to handle the entire mechanism of daily existence —food, cleaning, bills, buying, social duties, a dozen other preoccupations quite apart from rearing young—and all this *besides,* my dear male twin, whatever demands a chosen art or profession makes on us.

Now, I profoundly hope, no woman will accept this crazy imbalance, just as no man worth his humanity will accept the daily competitive grind of sole provider at the expense of loving and knowing and *being* with his wife and children, sharing the whole of life. Damn it, Wohleben, if we don't fuse in the basics of life, there won't *be* a life.

W: But yourself, as writer! there must be specific professional drawbacks in being a woman.

M: There are—there have been. I have turned down important jobs for one reason only: not to lose a man through frequent absence or change of place or public embarrassment, or conflicting interest, or greater prominence than his.

What might have been the chance of a lifetime for a man became a tortured choice for a woman.

W: Why were you so afraid? Did you think yourself indispensable to whatever man you lived with?

M: No. Just anchorless without him. And, in the light of that time, "un-female." Afraid to be judged "aggressive."

W: I should have been around more then.

M: You should.

I didn't have to tell Wohleben the smaller aggravations assailing a woman writer and speaker even at this presumably enlightened moment in time.

Had I been a male writer of equivalent professional stature, for instance, I would not have been repeatedly exposed in the press to the cliches of male semantics still blithely used by reviewers even in publications that should know better.

"Lady writers" (poets, novelists, critics). "The lady is under the apprehension that . . ." And so on, and so on. A small put-down, perhaps, but mean, demeaning, and so intended. What man would tolerate being called a "gentleman writer"?

These semantics include marked differences in words used to describe the same qualities. A critical, strong speech made by a man is "blunt" or "outspoken" or "pulls no punches." A speech of similar force and candor made by a woman is "waspish," "sarcastic," or "cutting." A man of strong opinions is defined as having "deep convictions." A woman so constituted is merely "opinionated," and always "aggressive."

This is doubled in spades by television which may dote on pretty entertainers, international female celebrities, and a few bright young women news reporters, but which harbors a deep aversion to controversial or authoritative females over forty. The gray temples and deepening furrows that are marks of distinction in Walter Cronkite or Eric Sevareid are on TV (and presumably to their audiences) marks of disaster in women of equal years and value: as fatal as the white crosses on the windows of abandoned houses.

For that matter, the editorial pages of the major newspapers of this country include no regular woman spokesman. Elsewhere, certainly, women as reporters, columnists, advice-givers, and gossip sifters. But the papers' mastheads are, with minimal exceptions, entirely composed of men, as are editorial decisions a male monopoly.

All this will undoubtedly change; is, hopefully, changing. But no woman writer who has worked through the last thirty years can deny what this exclusion has done to her in thwarting development and stature in her chosen field.

The kind of ruthless ambition that batters ceaselessly against these walls can sometimes breach them. But the cost of this fight is the diversion of vital forces which would otherwise flow into creation itself, and into the kind of personal humanity which should be invested in it. This price I have never wanted to pay.

So now, Wohleben, you have your answer. I have above all wanted to stay a human being. And if that is the reason why success has eluded me, I can blame the loss on no one else, including yourself.

• • •

What else does the last ghost know? has learned from the long parade of selves now merged and compacted into the final one?

First and foremost, as this chronicle tries to illuminate, human duality. Eight years ago, in a symposium on "The Potential of Women" in San Francisco, I proposed in a speech what I had long before felt to be true and what genetic science confirms: simply, "that each human being, male or female, is composed of both male and female components and that the proportion of one to the other varies widely in each person":

> While the public generally assumes that all "normal" women are, or should be, a hundred per cent female, the truth is that a woman can be seventy or even sixty per cent female to forty per cent male and still function biologically as a woman, with all the physical attributes this entails.
>
> Yet together with these functions and attributes, the woman with a higher quotient of masculine chromosomes must function also on other levels, whether it is in the world of ideas or performance or in the expression of sexual drives not necessarily linked to procreation. Such women can love men yet not submerge themselves

to them; can enjoy domesticity but not devote themselves to it; can be "feminine" but not make a fetish of it. In so being, they may miss the intense pleasures of submission, the unity of character and the security of role which the "normal" women enjoy, but they can also gain that breadth of experience, intellectual and emotional, that free and single identity which their majority of sisters are often denied. (And often deny themselves, out of fear.)

The argument—hardly revolutionary but still without public acceptance when it was made—added that everything said about such "dual" women applied as well to men:

. . . the non-competitors, the dreamers rather than the doers, the sensitive and gentle men who possess a higher-than-average proportion of female components without being in any sense effeminate. Equipped neither as fighters nor—primarily—as breadwinners, lacking the desire to impose their will on others or to dominate the women they love, they are in their own way as valuable to society as their "normal" aggressive brothers. And certainly less dangerous to the peace of the world.

This was a velvet glove. The mail gauntlet has now been thrown down by the Women's Liberation movement and the trumpet is no longer muted. Without this revolution no major social and political change, in the name of survival, can succeed.

Yet there are millions still in the realm called middle America who shut their ears to it, deride it, resist it, fear it; men and women who find the historic arrangement of the sexes convenient—however hollow—and safe—however insecure.

The burden of separate identity is very heavy: they prefer not to know themselves as they really are. It is easier not to. It is also easier to die than live.

Yet life demands that the duality in men and women be freed to function, released from hate or guilt. All wars derive from lack of empathy: the incapacity of one to understand and accept the likeness or difference of another. Whether in nations or the encounters of race and sex, competition then replaces compassion; subjection excludes mutuality.

Only through this duality in each can a man and woman have empathy for each other. The best lovers are men who can imagine and even feel the specific pleasures of women; women who know the passions and vulnerabilities of the penis —triumphant or tender—in themselves.

Without empathy, men and women, husbands and wives, become tools of each other: competitors, rivals, master and slave, buyer and seller. In this war the aggressions of the wholly "feminine" woman are just as destructive (mostly to the male) as the aggressions of the wholly "masculine" man.

For centuries the need to prove this image of masculinity has lain at the root of death: the killing of self and others in the wars of competition and conquest; the perversion of humanity itself.

We need each other's qualities if we are ever to understand each other in love and life. The beautiful difference of our biological selves will not diminish through this mutual fusion. It should indeed flower, expand; blow the mind as well as the flesh. When women can cherish the vulnerability of men as much as men can exult in the strength of women, a new breed could lift a ruinous yoke from both. We could both breathe free.

• • •

9.

With typical male vanity (Ha, Wohleben, you male chauvinist pig!) you keep reminding me that for a candid woman I have been very vague about your sex; talking about the presence of many men in my life but making no specific allusions.

Inherited maternal reticence? You should know better by now, my friend. About husbands, yes, for obvious reasons. About specific lovers, past, present, and living? Yes.

But I have never in my life had hang-ups about bodies, single or together, about the act of love (or copulation or, if you prefer, fucking), nor have I ever believed in what used to be called "unnatural practices." Nothing which human beings do to give or receive physical pleasure with each other is unnatural. I find all uses of the flesh except the infliction of cruelty or harm an affirmation of life, and pity men and women who lack the curiosity to explore them.

To write about them now when the puritan dam of repression has been totally breached would simply be—well—more water over it. Once more bad timing; too late. Too late to earn millions through detailed manuals of erotic technique, through personal revelations from Mr. Cock or Miss Cunt, through a spate of books and surveys that tell you all you ever wanted to know about sex except love.

If all these have produced a marvelous new release for society in the course of making the agents of liberation (usually non-writers) very rich, one can only be thankful. The visions of millions of marital mattresses bouncing in new-found ecstasies, of formerly neutered men and women at last being guaranteed orgasmic regularity, should certainly warm the cockles of other hearts besides their own.

Born too soon for such sanctioned delights, openly arrived at, a vast number of my own generation, especially women, have silently endured sexual deprivation through the shame and ignorance long fostered on them by puritan laws and the crippling proscriptions of the church.

I say women especially, because men have always been infinitely freer to explore the riches of the sexual empire than we: through mobility, through wide choice, through their simpler mechanism of release.

In body and psyche men are more vulnerable than women. Their frailer births and earlier deaths are supportive evidence of the former, while, in the latter they can exert no conscious control of their main organ of ego and source of pride, their cocks.

Because the complexity of the female organism is not overt, it demands far more knowledge and imagination from their male partners in sex than they usually get.

It has in fact, been a frequent source of surprise to me through my life that men choosing intercourse with a woman

—any woman—should know so little about her particular sexual mechanisms and the special needs of her body. Many men of superior intelligence and virility (these are not always paired) do not care enough either to discover them or cater to them. Now, hopefully, women are honest enough to tell them if they can't find out by themselves; even, perhaps, honest enough to tell them when their climax has not been shared.

But for so many centuries have women automatically assumed their lack of simultaneous orgasm to be their "fault" (or disability), that they have resorted to faking rather than confessing. And so many men have never known the difference.

A woman who loves men, aware of their intense vulnerability, would rather experience the immense pleasure of coition, of the presence of man ascendant in her, than, by acknowledging her aborted release, in some way diminish him. So she watches the sleeping, satisfied body of her lover while her own is awake and still in fiery need.

I have never seen the reverse. To know every need of a man, to explore it and cherish it, seems imperative. Awake, the cock is magnificent; asleep like a sleeping child. One studies every means of arousal, or rest, acutely aware of timing, mood, words, actions.

But many men are satisfied with less, prefer less. Have little patience for complexity in woman, especially if it matches their own. For many men, the sexual satisfaction of women is less a matter of love than pride: a reaffirmation of potency more than a gift of self. The deeper involvement of total empathy can frighten them, and I cannot blame them. Nor, for that matter, have I ever done so.

Long before *Playboy,* Woman was not the sum of her parts: her parts were her sum.

And if some of her non-physical parts were too much like their own, God help her, since men could not dominate her.

That is precisely why, my dear Wohleben, if I could not be a conductor, a scientist, or a statesman, I wished I could simply be a dumb broad with big breasts and no trace at all of you.

• • •

On second thought, though, I would have missed a very interesting life without you around. Even more so if we had been a peripatetic mistress rather than a wife. But, then, you nagged at me all along about that.

The only thing that you refused to realize was my delayed yet intensely domestic self. I loved making a home attractive, I loved a sense of serenity and sequence, I loved making a man comfortable, I loved feeding him. Yes, even that, though only, perhaps, because I had never (as millions of women still do) had to cook three meals a day, forever. But when I did cook it was because I loved not only the taste and smell of food but the preparing of it. For someone stuck at a typewriter—the least sensuous occupation in the world—the handling of fruits and vegetables and herbs and meats was physical release; a return to basic indulgence.

But then, we were both strongly animal, you and I. Why else did we dive through breakers and swim far out, if not for our pre-human origins in deep salt water? Why do we have to feel what we love—from sculpture to flesh and bone and hair—to know it? Why is nakedness such delight, why do the heads and necks and haunches of horses arouse such rapture? Or the high flight of gulls or small shining birds, or the trembling legs of fawns or one single round and perfect translucent stone?

Oh . . . marriage. How did I get from there to here? Ah yes—domestic food, the touch of things. Typical irrational female sequence, isn't it?

Well, one can share all these things in marriage, of course. But after a long look backward they might be shared, I think, in better ways between a man and a woman without any paper sanction or sacrament.

I don't know. Either I wasn't made for marriage, or marriage not for me—except for certain periods, at certain times. So long, I suppose, as I was wanted.

Even then I always resisted the business of being Mrs. Someone-or-Other. After three different tags, it got so that when a Mrs. Slotnik was paged in a public place I wasn't sure whether it was for me or not.

It certainly wasn't *me*. It was something I had to accept, but never liked. I breathed freely only under my own, my "professional" name.

Hoary idea, in any case, expecting a woman to surrender her name to her husband's in exchange for his. Why? Would any man submerge his identity and heritage to the woman he wed?

Ownership, of course: the ancient barter. The man possessing, the woman possessed (and protected). Deeded to him, like any house or object. For twenty years she is Mary Jones, overnight she is Mrs. Smith.

This sanctioned state of dependence goes much deeper than loss of name alone. She not only lives with her husband, but for him and through him. What a glorious cop-out from being herself! From *finding* herself!

And then, this deadly pairing: Mr. and Mrs., Mr. and Mrs., the animals two by two. What a social blight, a human deterrent!

The young know this. It's Mike and Jill and Rod and Joan, and who cares who lives with whom, or for how long, or whose child was born before—or out of—wedlock?

And what children really care which surname they bear (if they ever fill out forms), their mother's or their father's? Let them choose either. Let the continuity of both bloods be accepted and proclaimed.

Why only in queens? It's the natural human right. I loved my families, I was proud of their names. Why borrow a man's just because I live with him as legally paired?

Let those who will, marry—in the name of love or protection or children or live-in cooks, or a man's position and power. If they are happy, bless them.

I would choose live-in mistress, myself. No security there, no boredom either. Some separations, inevitably, but a discretion built on necessary lies. I would not expect a man to be continent on a three-week trip away from me, nor would I be, in all probability. I would merely not want to be told; or tell. Believing it to be a matter of purely sensual need; transient, dismissable. And when he came back (or I) we would notice no change in us or between us. That we wanted to live with each other should be enough. And when this wish died—well—who loves without pain?

Parting is bad enough; divorce is worse. So no, Wohleben. Change marriage, or leave it. For every happy marriage I have known, at least ten others are stifling habits or accommodations dragged into death, or broken—usually by the aging man in a gasp for life—or by his own death.

Why are you laughing, W.? (He says that in the wholly hypothetical event that a man I loved asked me to marry him, I would.)

Probably!

• • •

10.

A renewed freedom informed this final ghost. The adventurer stretched, the woman made love with no thought of bonds, the writer coiled for another spring.

The loneliness shared by an overwhelming number of women, at an age when they are given no other choice, was a frequent visitor; still is. But in some ways a beneficent one. It not only forces the revival of old resources left in abeyance, but the birth of new ones, both in thought and act. It also deepens the intensity of friendships with men and women which the nature of marriage—its very self-sufficiency—tends to reduce.

There is, too, in any viable marriage, an accommodation or abdication of will in many small things: a surveillance and also impingement of the other's moods and desires.

Now I could come and go as I wished; see whom I wanted; look as I chose; embarrass no one, since no one was responsible for me. When the spotlight shone, it dimmed no one else's lights.

These are small freedoms, often too frail to rout the demons of solitude and the tortures of self-doubt. The fact that there was a living to be earned, though, helped to blank them out. Monthly articles for *McCall's* provided most of my income for a year, and for one winter, in '67, professional ego was immensely gratified by a monthly essay on the editorial page of the New York *Times*. (It was correspondingly deflated by abrupt cancellation of the series in the fall. Too easy to read, perhaps?)

In 1967 the Center for the Study of Democratic Institutions invited me to the second Pacem in Terris Conference in Geneva: another doomed effort to end the war in Vietnam. No delegations were sent by the Soviet Union, North or South Vietnam, or by the State Department of the United States. But the majority of the world's other nations from Europe, Asia, and Africa were represented by individuals of exceptionally high caliber. And among the Americans who attended were Senators Fulbright, Clark, Pell and Brooke; Dr. Martin Luther King and James Farmer, John Kenneth Galbraith, Justice William O. Douglas, Dr. Linus Pauling, and at least a dozen more highly distinguished citizens whom I would otherwise not have had the privilege of meeting. Since Poland and East Germany were also represented, the chance of meeting and talking informally with Communist leaders was—at least to me—worth the trip alone.

As in all such conferences, many of the speeches were long, predictable, and hedged with the abstractions usually (and sadly) required by the protocol of official, if not personal, dialogue even at this clearly unofficial probe of attitudes and options. The ears back home, after all, were flapping.

At the end of the four-day session, the floor and the microphone was open to non-panel, non-spokesmen like myself: the listeners. We were allotted exactly five minutes to address the assemblage on any theme we chose.

Several of the liveliest, most hard-hitting comments enlivened this session; one more proof of the virtues of brevity.

My own comment began with the remark that no young at all were represented at this convocation since the median age seemed to range from forty to seventy.

Speaking of our absent American youth, I said:

They are deprived of the leaders they deserve. They have a President who speaks neither to them nor for them, who in fact profoundly offends them. They have a Vice-President who would rather be President than right. They have a Secretary of State who tells them nothing that they recognize as true. Only a few of their elected representatives—and the best of them are probably here—speak their language and give them hope.

Otherwise, these wise and tormented young have nowhere to turn. On the campuses they cry out against the war in Vietnam, they burn their draft cards, they court prison, they preach love not war, they are ready to sacrifice themselves for peace in a country where it is considered more patriotic to mourn a dead soldier than honor a living conscience.

Daily they perform acts of faith. They deserve such acts from us. They deserve political leaders who are prepared to burn their votes in defense of their beliefs. And some of them at this meeting may be doing just that.

They deserve representatives who will risk their whole careers rather than sanction catastrophe.

They deserve a country strong enough, and it is the strongest in the world, to perform that one act of trust which could open the only avenue to reason and peace, the end of bombing.

Nothing that they are told makes this exercise of power defensible because they know it is as futile as it is brutal.

The reception to this blast was loud, startled, but warm, and many foreign representatives—East, West, and African—along with compatriots, came to shake my hand.

The Center's subsequent report of the Pacem in Terris II remarked that "undoubtedly the most severe attacks on U.S. actions in Vietnam came from Americans themselves, notably from Linus Pauling, Reverend Martin Luther King, and Marya Mannes."

The day after mine (theirs had been earlier, scheduled speeches), the Executive Vice-President of the UN Association of the United States delivered a statement clearly in rebuttal (and rebuke) to it.

I patted my horse, and saw Wohleben grinning.

• • •

March 1971

Why stop there? Four years have gone by: years of work and pleasure overlaid, day after day, by a deepening horror at what we are doing to others abroad and to ourselves here.

To both of us—him and me—is the added pain (sometimes muted by a certain relief) that we are the last of a breed: the tag end of a civilization that seems to be going down the drain along with the other monumental waste, carrying us out to the last of the dumping grounds. Pollutants now, unredeemable, un-recyclable.

To our youthful contemporaries, presumably. "Out of My Time": what better synonym for Not With It? Because we are turned on more to Bach than Rock? To Rembrandt than Warhol? To Keats than Corso?

No, that's too easy. We are as much in phase (he and I) with the beauty of the naked young now as Praxiteles was. As much fired by imperative rebellion as we were in our own youth. As contemptuous of sham as any children born in any age.

But what we have seen and known and felt for many years cannot be put down as "irrelevant" because in terms of human development it is timeless.

The real irrelevance lies in the fad, the fashion, the cult, the frenzy—whether in art or living—which swallows the individual in the group. It is an abdication of independent judgment which can, at the least, diminish and at the worst brutalize.

Is it really possible, at last, to kill the "smile of reason" which has irradiated the whole of Western civilization from Plato to Jefferson, from Voltaire to Shaw? To destroy the structure of light and balance, the delicate scale of perception and justice that endures only through the disciplines of mind and heart?

While the young fight the official barbarism of unsentient power—the insanities of war and the ruinous priorities imposed by leaders and organizations in the *name* of reason, perhaps our last duty is to fight for the civilization *of* reason. What is killing it is a new barbarism in the name of "The People": an unfocused hate which, because the name has no meaning, can be exploited for the worst as well as the best of reasons.

The worst is the rejection of the concept of the superior human being, the civilized man. Without the standards that define his attributes, society falls apart. For they include among qualities of mind and heart and judgment, a code of civility and concern for others without which life for all becomes unlivable—as it nearly is now.

Is there time to raise an army for this cause? At seventy-two my father thought so, sickened even thirty years ago by the debasement of man:

"There are other ways beyond music of trying to bind mankind in a common fight against the overwhelming forces of materialism and greed, of intolerance and rapacity, but they all have this in common with music: that they are based on creation and not on destruction. That is why I mistrust such drastic means of changing the world and the spirit of man as revolution. For revolution is admitted to be, in the main, based on initial destruction: on a clearing of the ground, a razing of all things that were built through the generations, and the loss of this precious residue is seldom compensated by the new structure that replaces it."

"The precious residue." Worth saving? There's a very small army left to fight for it, and a weary one.

And with what weapons? Knowledge, experience, and passion are all we have left. Passion for a universal order that governs nature, man, and all living things. Passion for a continuity of human experience in which the past is not only vital to the present but without which there is no tolerable future.

The barbarian weapon is fission: the splitting asunder. It

has been perfected for death. Our only weapon is fusion: an imperfect process still, though designed for life.

Wohleben, for God's sake hurry and develop it in time. It's your business to discover, I to use.

Hurry.